SAN FRANCISCO PERFORMING ARTS LIBRARY AND MUSEUM JOURNAL, NO. 3

OAKLAND BALLET: THE FIRST 25 YEARS
1965–1990

BY WILLIAM HUCK

Foreword by Ronn Guidi

SAN FRANCISCO PERFORMING ARTS LIBRARY AND MUSEUM JOURNAL
No. 3
SPRING–SUMMER 1990

EDITOR: STEPHEN COBBETT STEINBERG
DESIGN DIRECTOR: CAL ANDERSON
PRODUCTION ARTIST: SARA ANDERSON
COMPOSITION: MARK WOODWORTH
PRINTING: ALANS, INC.

The JOURNAL is published twice a year by the San Francisco Performing Arts Library and Museum (formerly, the Archives for the Performing Arts). The subscription rate for 1990 is $20 (domestic); $30 (foreign). The JOURNAL is the successor to the Library's formerly quarterly, ENCORE. Back volume and single-issue prices available on request.

Address all correspondence and subscription orders to: JOURNAL, San Francisco Performing Arts Library and Museum, 399 Grove Street, San Francisco, CA 94102.

Any findings, opinions, or conclusions contained herein are those of the individual authors and not those of the Library or any of its funders.

US-ISSN-1047-4110

FRONT COVER: LYNN PENDLETON IN EUGENE LORING'S *BILLY THE KID*
INSIDE FRONT COVER: SHIRLEE REEVIE IN BRONISLAVA NIJINSKA'S *LES BICHES*
INSIDE BACK COVER: SUMMER LEE RHATIGAN IN JOHN BUTLER'S *CARMINA BURANA*
BACK COVER: COMPANY MEMBERS IN BRONISLAVA NIJINSKA'S *LES NOCES*

Contents

Foreword

1990 marks Oakland Ballet's twenty-fifth anniversary season. Amid all the celebrating, I took a deep breath, reflected, and thought to myself that our story really began long before the founding of the company in 1965. In fact, it may have begun as early as 1944 at Laurel Elementary School in Oakland.

One Thursday an event happened, insignificant to most other nine-year-olds, but truly life-shaping for me and what would eventually become Oakland Ballet. At 10:30 A.M. we had our Standard School Radio Broadcast. This was our music appreciation time, and that morning it was devoted to the music of Tchaikovsky. Our teacher passed around a brochure that explained something about the composer and his music. But it also had pictures, and one in particular of something I had never seen before in my short life. A beautiful woman was standing on her toes in a very short dress of white feathers, which made a circle around her waist. Her arms formed an oval shape above her head. Over her and slightly to the right was a man leaping; his legs were opened wide, almost in a split.

That one-half hour of music transported me to another world, as did the picture of the leaping man. With unusual determination, I told my teacher that I wanted to be that leaping man—a "want" that was to remain tucked away in my private world for a number of years.

The "leap" to junior high school was to be another awakening, certainly another connecting link to the future. In the seventh grade at Bret Harte Jr. High School, Mrs. Cordella Dare entered my life. She was the drama teacher, student counselor, and worker of magic. It was with her that the tucked-away "want" was given new impetus, encouragement, and understanding. The dancing lessons began, and so did my insecure lifelong journey into the world of art.

Oakland High School was the next rite of passage, where order and chaos were unlikely friends. The "order" was provided by Mr. Hudson, my high school drama teacher, who continued to open doors (and sometimes pushed me through them) when the journey into the chaotic world of theater and dance seemed too foreboding. He prepared me for survival in the 1950s when a dance career was rare indeed. In spite of the times at hand, I had this intense desire to dance.

BY RONN GUIDI

5

Ronn Guidi founded the Oakland Ballet in 1965 and three years later opened the Oakland Ballet Academy, the primary training ground for future Oakland Ballet dancers. He has contributed more than forty works to the Company's repertory.

KURT JOOSS'S THE GREEN TABLE

My dance teacher during those years, Raoul Pausé, was a unique combination of iconoclasm and orthodoxy. Though he was an early pupil of Adolph Bolm of Diaghilev's Ballets Russes, he was also a student of Mary Wigman and Harald Kreutzberg. His dances had the discipline and freedom of both classical ballet and modern dance. His exploration of both idioms was rare for its time. Raoul Pausé was, in some ways, an enigma to me. An air of mystery surrounded him. He took me on a whirlwind journey of performances from musical theater to dance of the most dramatic nature. It seemed that the physical, spiritual, and artistic aspects of dance were so intertwined in his hands. It was in his studio that dancing became the ritual, the metaphor, and the magic—giving my life meaning and purpose.

Next came the "leap" into college, where dance and studies were definitely at odds. But it was the dancing that for me gave all things perspective. After graduation and my being drafted into the army, I was sent to Europe. Soon I found myself on a ship recrossing the Atlantic, homeward-bound (but not so prodigal).

Returning to Raoul's studio in 1961, standing at my favorite place at the barre, brought me a regained sense of comfort. And the next four years would be a time of concentrated exploration, when choreography would pour out of me: *Harp Concerto, Trois Gymnopédies, Canticle, Respighi Dances,* and *Hansel and Gretel* (in its original form). The years of apprenticeship had served me well and my art was coming to at least a modest fruition.

The year 1965 was the year for the "big leap"—the "grand jeté," so to speak. Founding Oakland Ballet was truly choosing a path toward an abyss of uncertainty. I felt as though my feet were planted firmly in midair. I was familiar with choreography and performing, but not with costume construction, lighting, advertising, payroll, marketing, balancing budgets, forming a board of directors, and talking to funders. Necessity and desire, however, are great motivators . . . and so I learned.

Opening a school in 1968 was a natural and exciting step toward the further fulfillment of Oakland Ballet. My right hand, and the day-to-day organizer of my life, was a remarkable woman—Betty Lewis. For the last fourteen years of her life, she dedicated all her energies to the school, the company, and me. Also at that time another remarkable woman walked into my life, Judy Ciraolo. To this day she continues to support the company and me, especially in unique artistic projects.

It is now twenty-five years since the founding of Oakland Ballet, an adventure that has become my life's work. In retrospect, I'm not sure when I began the search for my artistic roots—or heritage, if you will. But in a word, it led directly to Diaghilev. Producing his art as a living repertoire for my company was the natural consequence of this search, this journey. Today, the repertoire includes many masterpieces of that incredible era: *Sheherazade, Polovetsian Dances, Les Sylphides, Les Noces, Les Biches, Le Train Bleu, Petrouchka.* Dance was never the same after Diaghilev. His world of art produced the great choreographers of our century: Michel Fokine, Léonide Massine, Bronislava Nijinska, and George Balanchine. Their art lives in Oakland Ballet, as well as in the second flowering of choreographers: Agnes de Mille, Antony Tudor, Eugene Loring, Kurt Jooss, Anna Sokolow, and Ruthanna Boris. At the forefront of taking dance into the twenty-first century are our contemporary choreographers: Tandy Beal, Val Caniparoli, Carlos Carvajal, Betsy Erickson, Emily Keeler, John McFall, David McNaughton, Tomm Ruud, Ron Thiele, and Brenda Way. Speaking to us of our own time and times past, these artists are a living legacy of Oakland Ballet.

Trust, belief, dedication, sacrifice, and generosity have given life to the Oakland Ballet. Dancers and staff have been so dedicated; the board of directors so believing; banks so trusting; the City of Oakland, Alameda County, the California Arts Council, the National Endowment for the Arts, and numerous corporations, foundations, and private citizens so generous. With them *all*, the reality of Oakland Ballet has been achieved.

Through twenty years of this adventure has been my friend, dancer, choreographer, conscience, and Associate Artistic Director, Ron Thiele. As baseball player turned dancer, he has gone to bat for this company above and beyond the call of duty. I am so grateful for his steadfastness.

This book, *The First Twenty-Five Years*, is an account of a unique artistic journey with countless audiences, artists, dancers, friends, and supporters. And, I must tell you, there is much more adventure ahead! I am so thankful that this book has been written by someone whose hands dance across the pages, bringing to life the real life story of a grass-roots company.

Acknowledgments

Dance is the most ephemeral of the arts, the most difficult to chronicle and document. Writing dance history is thus frequently problematic, because dance rarely leaves behind a full set of records. This history of the Oakland Ballet would not have been possible without the help of many people who were themselves participants in this history, and who graciously consented to be interviewed: Mark Denton, Ronn Guidi, Lance James, Tricia Kaye, Dianne Brock King, Michael Lowe, Ron Thiele, Patrice Whiteside, and Stephanie Zimmerman.

I should also like to thank Millie Mitchell, Oakland Ballet's hard-working Director of Marketing/Communications, for her tireless support and co-operation. David Gere, music and dance critic of the *Oakland Tribune*, provided valuable insights into the Company's history, and also facilitated my use of the *Tribune's* library. Paul Parish, the Bay Area correspondent for *Ballet Review*, generously shared his knowledge of the Company with me as well.

For his vital encouragement and masterful editing of my manuscript, I should also like to thank Stephen Cobbett Steinberg.

And lastly, Steven Anderson deserves my heartfelt gratitude for his constant support.

This publication has been made possible, in part, with generous support from the Walter and Elise Haas Fund, Judy and Mike Ciraolo, and the Oakland Ballet Association. This issue is sponsored by SF PALM's Dance Research Center, which is funded, in part, by the Andrew W. Mellon Foundation and the Dance Program of the National Endowment for the Arts, a federal agency.

BY WILLIAM HUCK

William Huck is a dance and music critic whose writings have appeared in many publications, including "The Los Angeles Times," "Opera Quarterly," "The San Francisco Chronicle," and "The San Francisco Sentinel." Since 1984, he has served as the program editor for the "San Francisco Ballet Magazine." He is the author of "San Francisco Symphony: Seventy-Five Years of Music."

RON THIELE AND SUMMER LEE RHATIGAN IN
MICHEL FOKINE'S *SHEHERAZADE*

Prelude: The Americanization of Dance

In the last twenty-five years, the United States has experienced a dance boom that has seen a blossoming of talent, an almost incredible surge of energy, and the building of a truly national audience for ballet and modern dance. Many observers, looking at this extraordinary phenomenon from the outside, have traced its source to a single man, George Balanchine, who brought the art of moving to music to a refinement surpassing even that of Imperial Russia. They have dated its beginnings to the flood of money the Ford Foundation began distributing in the early sixties, and they have accounted for its continuing appeal by pointing to those wonderfully charismatic Russian defectors who lit up the balletic heavens during the sixties and seventies.

All of these factors, no doubt, helped to fuel the tremendous blaze of America's love affair with dance. But they did not start the fire, nor were they, really, its sustaining force. The spark came from America itself, from mothers willing to drive their sons and daughters to ballet classes all across the nation, and from teachers who, having received the sacred flame from Diaghilev-era dancers, were willing to endure poor pay and cramped quarters for the privilege of transmitting that love to a rising generation of dancers.

The dance boom is thus the story of countless studios, run on a shoestring in the late forties and fifties. It began in those little pageants watched mainly by the students' relatives. In time these spectacles became ballets, as the young dancers gained technique and confidence. With this change came also a growing audience. Slowly the nation, freed from Victorian prudery and now open to the magic of movement, discovered dance. But we could not have done so without the dancers who grew up in a darker, more restricted era. We owe the dance boom not to one choreographer, a single foundation, or a few glamorous defectors, but to the many hometown students who learned a taste for dance as children and kept that love steadfastly into adulthood.

The Oakland Ballet, which celebrated its twenty-fifth anniversary in

RAOUL PAUSE

the fall of 1990, was created by just such individuals. Its history is the tale of America's great dance boom seen from the inside, from the perspective of men and women dedicated to ballet above all else.

When it began in 1965, the Oakland Ballet was composed of a modest handful of dancers, led by Ronn Guidi, still the Company's guiding light. At any given performance there were rarely more than four adult performers, who each received $10 a concert, in addition to a few bright and shiny-faced adolescents who wanted to become dancers.

Most of the new company's performances were actually in-school demonstrations, featuring Guidi himself, Dianne Brock, and Arthur Conrad. But these modest outings should not be sniffed at, for they were a crucial part of the building not only of the Oakland Ballet, but also of America's increasing appetite for dance. Throughout its first eight years, the Company danced on postage-stamp-sized stages, in churches that barely had a stage, and in gymnasiums where the janitors proudly polished the floor to a superhigh gloss and an equally supertreacherous finish. It was a time when the dancers sewed their own costumes, mothers made posters, Guidi sold tickets before changing into his dance clothes, and, in short, everybody did everything. The Oakland Ballet began as a truly community-involved organization, acquiring a feeling and atmosphere that even the thriving and sophisticated institution of today has not completely lost.

In 1985, when the Oakland Ballet visited New York's Brooklyn College for the second time, Anna Kisselgoff of the *New York Times* spoke accurately when she noted that "The Oakland Ballet from California is a fine and rare example of a so-called regional company that has pulled itself up by its artistic bootstraps."[1] Today Oakland Ballet has a working repertory of over fifty ballets, which includes such distinguished works as Bronislava Nijinska's *Les Noces*, Agnes de Mille's *Fall River Legend*, and Kurt Jooss's *The Green Table*, as well as a host of works by contemporary California choreographers. The Company currently gives more than sixty-two performances each season, thirty at home and thirty-two on tour in twenty-two cities nationwide. It has visited Europe; attracts a public that reaches into the hundreds of thousands; and has been featured on the cover of several national dance publications.

This astonishing development has come primarily from the inspiration of one man, Ronn Guidi, the Company's founding director. He has seen the Oakland Ballet through struggle and success; his vision has shaped its dancers and molded its repertory. The story of the Oakland Ballet is also his story, which, like the Company's, began long ago in one of the hundreds of nearly anonymous ballet studios that brought us America's dance boom.

When a 1948 fire swept through the dance studio that Raoul Pausé had made out of an old stable,[2] the elegant dancer-teacher-choreographer did not have the funds to rebuild. Instead he simply moved his small company and school to a new locale above an auto parts store at 4689 Telegraph Avenue in the heart of Oakland. There, six days a week, students climbed a steep, narrow staircase, past a life-size portrait of a flamenco dancer and into the big, light-filled room. About the room were pictures of Pausé, "in striking poses, often in natural settings and showing a lot of skin," as one of his most gifted pupils remembered.[3] At the far end stood a small platform raised about a foot above the studio floor. It was from that insignificant stage that Raoul Pausé molded the minds, the bodies, and the spirits of the dancers who would later form the Oakland Ballet.

Even in 1990 one can sense the legacy of Raoul Pausé in the Company's eclectic repertory and its emphasis on the dramatic and the impassioned over the precise and the cold. Pausé, who was forty-one years old at the 1948 opening of his new studio, inscribed a motto on one of his next performance programs that summed up both his life work and the legacy he left: "The Dance, whether Classical or Modern, rigid or free, always depicts some facet of life, whether light in mood, heavy in theme, significant or fanciful."[4]

Lean and smoothly muscled, with an old-world elegance about him, Pausé combined grace and fire. Anita Paciotti, a Pausé pupil and one of Oakland Ballet's early ballerinas, remembers her old master fondly: "There was a lot of philosophy in his classes, for he believed that dancing was a response of the total personality. He was a naturalist with a strict, natural diet long before it was fashionable, and he gave the appearance of being tall because he had the straightest posture I have ever seen. His bright blue eyes commanded your immediate attention. In all, he was the most graceful man I ever knew; I can still see him drawing out his turns ever so slowly."[5]

Pausé was not interested in the outward signs of classroom discipline. Students did not have to wear black leotards or pink tights; they came dressed in whatever practice clothes they owned. Nor was he interested in the superficial discipline of classical ballet, which he described as just "display dancing."[6] Instead he emphasized the meaning, the passion behind

one's gestures. "While his own form was always true," Paciotti recalls, "he never concentrated his teaching on the classical elements of form. We didn't practice our turnout, or pointing our feet, or squeezing our feet into a perfect fifth—at least not particularly. Ballet's basic steps were all there, but when he wanted you to point your feet harder or get your leg higher, he wouldn't tell you to do so, but instead say, 'Light the light inside.' It was the inside light that mattered to Raoul."[7]

There was both a softness and an immediacy to Pausé's teachings. For him the arms were always rounded. He was not looking for the long, angular gestures or the tight, energized positions favored by Balanchine; his ideal was the inward peace of gracefully held poses and flowing movements. Whereas for Balanchine the question was almost how fast a dancer could do his combinations, for Pausé it was conversely almost how slow. When demonstrating a pirouette, for example, he would sometimes put a record on his head to show how, if the dancer's posture was kept straight, the propulsion of the turn should not make the record slip. The reason Pausé could demonstrate the smoothness of a pirouette with a record balanced on his head was that he invariably used records rather than a pianist in his classroom and rehearsals.

Pausé's classroom methodology naturally reflected his training. Born in Chicago, the dancer had moved early in his life to Oakland. At the age of fourteen the *Oakland Tribune* named him one the area's most promising juveniles.[8] At fifteen Pausé returned to Chicago and began his professional career dancing with the Chicago Civic Opera Ballet, then directed by the famous Diaghilev dancer Adolph Bolm. Under Bolm's tutelage, Pausé got his first taste of an aesthetic that concentrated on story ballets with strong narrative situations, exotic locales, and striking character dancing. In Chicago Pausé also came under the spell of the Pavley-Oukrainsky Ballet, whose corps he joined at sixteen. Andreas Pavley and Serge Oukrainsky, the two Russian émigré leaders of the troupe, had an unusual idea of ballet, formed by a mixture of the avant-garde aesthetics of pre-Revolutionary Russia, the extravagant chic of Paris fashion houses, and the bursting iconoclasm of America's roaring twenties.[9] Pausé brought this exotic influence back to Oakland when he returned in 1928 to set up the first of his various studios. Only two European trips in the mid-thirties to study with the modern dance masters Mary Wigman and Harald Kreutzberg, and a few small tours with dancers he had trained in Oakland, ever took him away again from his beloved city and his classroom.

It was at Pausé's Telegraph Avenue studio one day in 1950 that Ronn Guidi, a small, fourteen-year-old boy of Italian descent, appeared asking for instruction in ballet. The son of a former bantamweight boxer, now a Fremont Chevrolet plant worker, the boy came from a long-time Oakland family that also ran Blanche's Coffee Shop on MacArthur Boulevard. Guidi had first encountered ballet in the third grade. "At the Laurel Elementary School," he recalls, "our teacher had us listen to the Standard Hour radio broadcasts of classical music every Thursday. To keep our attention focused, she always passed around a printed program about the music. Each was nicely illustrated, and one time, when the broadcast included music from *Swan Lake*, there was a picture of a man leaping high into the air above a beautiful woman standing *en pointe*. Later that day I told my teacher that I wanted to be like that man."[10]

As Guidi now remembers, "at first I was the shy, quiet kid in the back row, the one least likely to succeed. But gradually Pausé drew me out, for he was responsible not only for my dance training, but also my artistic education—my outlook on life. So many ballet teachers train their students to look only at the steps and miss the meaning of a ballet as art. I remember that once Raoul bought me a ticket to see Margot Fonteyn in *Swan Lake*. When I came back and talked to him about it, I said, 'You know, she hopped on a pirouette.' So he bought me another ticket and said, 'Now go back and see the ballet.' It was a lesson I never forgot."[11]

By 1953 Pausé had associated himself and his dancers with Oakland's outdoor Woodminster Amphitheater, where he was in charge of directing and choreographing the musical numbers for the Oakland Light Opera Association. In the following year Guidi found himself on stage for the group's performance of a spectacle-ballet called *Magic Journey*. "With a cast largely composed of Pausé's pupils," reported the *Oakland Tribune*, "a few of whom seemed to be as young as four or five, [*Magic Journey*] was obviously intended to appeal primarily to youngsters. . . . The Pausé Ballet boasted some exceptionally capable adult performers . . . , including Pausé himself. Others whose work was impressive were Pat Marshall, Wendy Brophy, Ronn Guidi and Marc Wilde. . . . Although *Magic Journey* would never be mistaken for a professional production, it was completely charming in its current Woodminster presentation and will prove most satisfactory summer fare for both adults and their small fry."[12]

By 1957 Pausé had intensified his efforts by forming the Oakland Players Guild, which debuted at the Telegraph Avenue studio on August 5.[13] The two substantial works on the program were *Handful of Dust*, choreographed by Marc Wilde, and *Eye of Darkness*, by Pausé. Wilde's ballet was a dance tragedy about two sisters, one blind but blithe, the other sighted but bitter, while Pausé's work was a retelling of the Greek myth about Orpheus and Eurydice. Though the Guild announced only upcoming dance performances, the Company expressed the hope that it would soon expand "into other aspects of art expression, including drama and musicals."[14]

During the next seven years, Pausé's various companies were known by several "floating" names, including the Pausé Ballet, the California Ballet Company, and finally the most direct ancestor of the Oakland Ballet, the Oakland Civic Ballet, which debuted on Friday, November 25, 1960.[15] The next year, Guidi, who had not been present for the formation of the Oakland Civic Ballet due to a two-year stint in the army in West Germany and a year dancing with the Nuremburg Opera Ballet, returned to Oakland and Pausé's classes. "At first, it was simply to keep my body in shape. I had no intention of dancing professionally, but instead thought I would return to being a schoolteacher as I had been for four months before being drafted."[16] Using his degree in Dramatic Literature from the University of California at Berkeley, Guidi had, in fact, secured a job teaching fourth grade in the Oakland public schools, but he could not escape the lure of the dance world, and soon produced his first choreography. That first ballet, premiered in 1961, was called *Harp Concerto*, set to a Handel concerto.[17] It was neoclassical in form, without content or story, as was the prevailing style of the time.

Harp Concerto, though not particularly notable in itself, opened the gates. In his second ballet, set to Erik Satie's *Trois Gymnopédies* and named after the music, Guidi showed his real abilities. For Anita Paciotti, this work proved the old maxim that if an artist has talent, the essence of it is there at the beginning. Guidi himself is proudest of a compliment he received from Alexandra Baldina, who danced the prelude in the first Diaghilev performance of Fokine's *Les Sylphides*. In the early sixties Baldina saw the ballet and perceptively observed, "You are a very interesting young man, for you give us an abstract ballet, which in the final moments you make into a story with a few, simple gestures."[18] Baldina had struck an important chord, for, like his teacher, Pausé, Guidi saw ballet always in terms of human drama. In America in the sixties and seventies Balanchine's more austere aesthetic, which stripped ballet of its dramatic stories and illustrative costumes, reigned supreme and made the Pausé-Guidi philosophy suspect, as if these ballet dramatists somehow cheapened a glorious and intellectual art form. But Guidi's path had been set by his esteemed teacher; much of the artistic history of the Oakland Ballet can be traced to Ronn Guidi's sometimes tentative, sometimes forthright, but always active search for his roots in dramatic dance.

Ronn Guidi—seen here with early Oakland Ballet dancers Dianne Brock and Anita Paciotti—began his dance training at age fourteen, under the instruction of Raoul Pausé. "He was responsible not only for my dance training, but also my artistic education —my outlook on life," Guidi recalls. "So many ballet teachers train their students to look only at the steps and miss the meaning of ballet as art."

A Company Is Formed

As the early sixties progressed, Ronn Guidi gradually took over more and
more of the responsibilities associated with the Oakland Civic Ballet.
Eventually this brought him into philosophic conflict with his teacher, for
Raoul Pausé had long cherished a dream that was larger than just ballet.
Trained as he was in the Chicago Opera Ballet, Pausé saw dance not only as
its own medium but as part of a more encompassing show. During his
career, he had frequently staged light opera and musicals, and maintained
his interest in drama as well.[1] In April 1962, Pausé fulfilled part of this
dream when he joined with Mark Fidler in taking over the old Foothill
Theater and turned it into the California Playhouse. As Fidler explained to
the *Oakland Tribune*: "Mr. Pausé and I hope to keep the theater going on a
year-round basis, every day. We will stage dance recitals, operas, as well as
musicals and drama."[2] Though Fidler graciously placed dance first on his
list of the theater's activities, the directors chose to open their venture
with *Oklahoma!*, followed by *The Pleasure of His Company*.

As Pausé put more and more of his energy into this plan for a
comprehensive performing arts theater, the dancers of the Oakland Civic
Ballet began to feel "like the step-children of the company."[3] In 1962 and
1963, public ballet performances became scarcer. As Guidi saw it, "The
theater was an expensive place to maintain, and Raoul's interests turned
more to the relatively lucrative field of musical comedies. Eventually I
could see the handwriting on the wall: Raoul was older than we thought,
and tired. If we stayed with him, there never was going to be a professional
ballet company devoted solely to dance."[4]

Despite the growing number of performances by the Oakland Civic
Ballet in 1964 and the first half of 1965, Guidi was determined on his
course. On September 15, 1965, Guidi, along with Robert A. Edgren,
Margaret Davis, Francine Darrah, and Barbara J. Edgren, formally executed
the Articles of Incorporation for a nonprofit organization to be called the
Oakland Ballet Company and Guild. These articles promised to "establish
and maintain . . . a skilled and competent company as an artistic and

RONN GUIDI AND ANITA PACIOTTI IN
HANSEL AND GRETEL

cultural contribution to the residents of the City of Oakland and its neighboring cities."[5]

Within ten days, the Company was in full swing with a performance at the Little Theater in Berkeley on September 25 and a pair of concerts at the Kaiser Center Auditorium on October 15 and 16. Reporting on that first concert in *Dance News*, Tom Borek unconsciously acknowledged the continuity between the old and the new by using the Company's new name, the Oakland Ballet, but calling these concerts the group's fifth season.[6] Indeed, those fall programs, featuring works by Pausé, Marc Wilde, and Angene Feves, were essentially the same as the concerts given by the Oakland Civic Ballet the previous spring.[7]

Nonetheless something different had happened: Ronn Guidi had left his fourth-grade classroom and was now in sole charge of the artistic development of the Oakland Ballet. "I finally had to decide whether I wanted art or security," Guidi has written. "I really wanted both, but I couldn't have that, so I settled for art."[8] Guidi had also found a new studio for his company on Foothill Boulevard. The one new ballet on those September–October programs was another definite sign of things to come. *Uirapuru*, Guidi's Brazilian fantasy about a bird (danced by a woman) who is transformed into a handsome man (danced by a man) and murdered when he falls in love with the beautiful maiden who had unwittingly caused his transformation, represented Guidi's reaching out for his own voice, with themes based on the unexplainable entanglements of love. As Guidi declared at the time: "Our long-range goal [for the Oakland Ballet] is to search out new avenues of dance. This week we're performing Villa-Lobos' twentieth century *Uirapuru* in dance, just as I used William Russell's and Lou Harrison's avant-garde music for the primitive rituals of *Canticles* earlier this year. I definitely feel that the discovery of new ballet music and the use of avant-garde or contemporary music is a responsibility."[9]

One aspect of the almost unbroken line connecting Pausé's company and Guidi's was the use of Marc Wilde's choreography. In the years after incorporation, Wilde—a former Pausé student and long his leading male dancer—was the Oakland Ballet's single most important choreographer besides Guidi himself. All the dancers liked working with him, for Wilde was witty and charming, spontaneous but also organized, and always inspiring. "Where Raoul was the patriarch, a very elegant man, lyrical and classic, Marc, who could also be very lyrical, had a much more enthusiastic personality," observes Dianne Brock, Oakland Ballet's first star ballerina. "Raoul's choreography was made up of nuances and subtleties, but Marc's dances were always filled with tremendous energy. When I think of the difference, I see it in terms of painting; whereas Raoul's was French impressionism with muted colors and delicate outlines, Marc's was German expressionism with broader strokes and bigger, splashier colors."[10]

Matching the old influence was a new one. In the spring of 1965 Angene Feves, who had been trained in Los Angeles by Gene Marinaccio, joined the Company and choreographed a commedia dell'arte ballet, *The Proposal of Pantalone*. Feves's importance, however, was not as a choreographer, but as dancer and teacher. While Ronn Guidi continued to teach class very much in the style of Raoul Pausé, spicing his combinations with philosophical observations and putting the emphasis on the meaning behind the steps, Feves concentrated on the building blocks of ballet. As part of her warm-up exercises, Feves followed the Marinaccio method of having the dancers stretch their muscles on the floor to enhance their turn-out. The idea was that by putting the dancers on the floor and removing the force of gravity, the dancers could develop a flexiblity unattainable through the barre and center exercises of the usual ballet class.

As Christmas neared, the Company was fully and completely the Oakland Ballet, but once again it continued tradition rather than breaking with it. In 1963 Guidi had collaborated with Pausé on the first version of what would become a perennial Oakland Ballet favorite, *Hansel and Gretel*. The ballet, based on the familiar story of two lost children threatened by the pie-baking witch, used substantial portions of Engelbert Humperdinck's opera on the same subject, as well as a collage of other music that in its first edition included snippets from Ferdinand Hérold's ballet *La Fille Mal Gardée* and the *Autumn Overture* by Edvard Grieg.[11] Ronn Guidi has explained his idea: "When I was in Germany, *Hansel and Gretel* was the ballet traditionally given at Christmas time. So when I returned to Oakland, I decided that we would do the same, and our version of Grimm's fairy tale was born. . . . Children really identify with Hansel and Gretel. They are truly frightened by the Wicked Witch and cheer for the happy ending. It happens all the time."[12]

Not only did children love *Hansel and Gretel*, but their parents did, too. Critics, soaked in Christmas *Nutcrackers*, especially appreciated the

During the early sixties, Ronn Guidi took over more and more of the responsibilities from his teacher and mentor, Raoul Pausé. Ready to form his own company, Guidi established the Oakland Ballet, which gave its first performances on September 25, 1965, in Berkeley. Guidi was the Company's artistic director as well as one of its principal choreographers and dancers (below and opposite, bottom). In 1968, Guidi also opened the Oakland Ballet Academy (opposite, top), the primary training ground for future Company dancers.

21

change of pace, as did the dancers. Tricia Kaye, who joined the Oakland company in 1971, has said that "after I danced Ronn's *Hansel,* I never wanted to do *The Nutcracker* again. It seemed so pallid and stiff next to Ronn's ballet, bursting with fun and originality."

Perhaps *Hansel and Gretel's* appeal to the innocent and the naive was not only the source of its success, but an explanation of Oakland Ballet's initial achievements as well. As Dianne Brock has said, "Ronn's early work was particularly attractive to children, which may have accounted for the way the Company was able to develop. Dance audiences in those days—in Oakland in particular—were not terribly sophisticated, and since Ronn was learning his own style too, it was a happy melding. The audience and the Company grew up together."

In December 1965, Anita Paciotti and Dianne Brock alternated as Gretel, Ronn Guidi danced Hansel, Angene Feves was both the Princess Flower and the Angel who saves the children. Following the German tradition, the evil witch, Rosina Rubylips, was played *en travesti* by Arthur Conrad, who came to ballet from the theater where he had worked as both actor and director. Conrad, who "never finished a single ballet class in his life," had an infectious good humor, a keen eye, and what Dianne Brock calls "his tremendous musicality."[13] This combination made Conrad the most important character dancer in the history of the Oakland Ballet, and Rosina Rubylips was his most famous role. As one reviewer put it, "[Conrad's] jagged leaps and clawing gestures portrayed the sorceress as the epitome of evil, while his unflagging bounce injected enormous verve into the production."[14]

When Oakland Ballet did its accounting at the end of its first fall-winter season, the books showed a positive balance of $19.71. Income (from donations, performances, and demonstrations) was listed as $4,220.10; expenditures (for costumes, equipment, advertising, dancers' expenses, printing, photos, postage, and miscellaneous) came to $3,747.64, with an additional accounts payable for auditorium rental and technicians in December of $452.75. Major donations had come in from Executive Aviation, the City of Oakland, and Kaiser Industries Corporation. In its first outings, the Company had been reviewed by Paul Hertelendy of the *Oakland Tribune,* Tom Borek of *Dance News,* and Russell Hartley of *Dance Magazine* for its performances at the Kaiser Center Auditorium, the Oakland Auditorium Theatre, the On Stage, the Berkeley Little Theater, and the Washington High School auditorium in Fremont. In the upcoming year, the Company would expand the radius of its activities to include the Bay Area communities of San Jose, San Leandro, and Walnut Creek.[15]

Despite these increased performing opportunities, all was not bright for Oakland Ballet. For one thing, the most substantial part of its income came not from public performances but from lecture-demonstrations that Ronn Guidi, Dianne Brock, and Arthur Conrad gave to students groups in elementary, junior high, and high schools throughout the area.[16] Secondly, opposition soon arose between the new company and Vern Nerden's Ballet Arts Foundation, which in 1965 had changed its name to Oakland Metropolitan Ballet. Guidi maintained that since Nerden's studios were in San Leandro and Alameda, Nerden's company was not truly part of the Oakland scene and had no right to the new name. The disagreement would have been a petty, senseless squabble, but for rumors from the City Council chamber that the city was in a position to fund only one ballet company, not two.[17]

Gradually, Guidi became discouraged. Perhaps the break with Pausé, though amicable on both sides, was psychologically more difficult than Guidi had anticipated. Whatever the cause, from 1966 until 1969, Guidi created no new choreography for the Oakland Ballet. Instead the director searched out other alternatives. In June 1967, for example, the two contending Oakland companies took a tentative step toward merger, when they presented a joint program that included Alan Howard's new version of *Swan Lake, Act II*, Nerden's *Task Force Nine, Jeux d'Enfants*, and the *Don Quixote Pas de Deux*, together with Guidi's *Trois Gymnopédies*. Though this merger never did work out, the very discussion of it was a sign of the Oakland Ballet's perilous condition.

Meanwhile, Guidi let his own company languish, showing *Trois Gymnopédies* and *Canticles* on Alan Howard's Pacific Ballet programs instead. In June 1968 he choreographed his delightful antiwar spoof, *The Incredibility Gap*, again for Pacific Ballet. The work, planned in cooperation with Country Joe and the Fish, came complete with hippies bearing picket signs, a caricatured Texas-style LBJ, and representatives of the Love Generation on LSD. When Guidi choreographed his next piece, again he did not return to his own company, but went instead to the San Francisco Ballet, for whom he made *Sun Music*, to a recent score by Australian composer Peter Schulthorpe. Depicting both the pleasant and

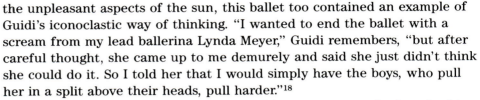

During its early years, one of the Oakland Ballet's leading choreographers was Marc Wilde (opposite, top), one of Raoul Pausé's students and long his lead dancer. Wilde has given the Company several of his most popular works, including "Bolero" and "Afternoon of a Faun," seen here with Stacey Swaner (below) and Robert Warner (opposite, bottom).

the unpleasant aspects of the sun, this ballet too contained an example of Guidi's iconoclastic way of thinking. "I wanted to end the ballet with a scream from my lead ballerina Lynda Meyer," Guidi remembers, "but after careful thought, she came up to me demurely and said she just didn't think she could do it. So I told her that I would simply have the boys, who pull her in a split above their heads, pull harder."[18]

Part of Guidi's discouragement with his own company had no doubt come from the Company's inability to keep its best dancers. Both Anita Paciotti and Sven Knorrlander, for example, had moved to the San Francisco Ballet, while Angene Feves had established her own company and school in Walnut Creek.

Amid these troubling doldrums there were two rays of hope for the Oakland Ballet—one external and one internal. Gerhard Samuel, conductor and director of the Oakland Symphony, believed in the fledgling company. Not only did Samuel program concerts with the Ballet on Oakland Symphony's Chamber Orchestra series, but he personally needled Guidi and kept telling him that what he needed was not to abandon his company but to get it off the Kaiser Auditorium's postage-stamp-size stage.[19] Even more important to the stability of the Company was the opening of the Oakland Ballet Academy on March 4, 1968. The Academy's curriculum offered classes for both children and adults, from beginners (with no previous experience) to advanced and professional dancers, as well as preballet classes for the very young. The new school boasted Guidi's personal supervision and guest teachers ranging from Grace Doty (long the prima ballerina of Pacific Ballet), to Sven Knorrlander, Arthur Conrad (whose specialty was mime), and Angene Feves. The school, which ironically flourished when the Company floundered, represented a major commitment by Guidi to the longevity of his struggling institution.[20]

Teaching now became a passion with Guidi, who found outlets not only at the Company's Academy but also as director of dance at both the University of California, Berkeley, and Merritt College. It was from these classes that the Company's renewal came. One particularly harried Wednesday in the fall of 1969, a tall, handsome, big-shouldered baseball player accompanied a soccer buddy to Guidi's UC ballet class. Ron Thiele had injured his arm and was looking for a way to improve his coordination and get back in shape. Not your ordinary college jock, Thiele was majoring in psychology and had sought artistic expression as a youth in painting and poetry. But nothing clicked until he sauntered into that ballet class at the age of twenty. Immediately Thiele was hooked, and Ronn Guidi had the makings of his first major male star, a dancer who believed so completely in the art of ballet that he would soon become the Company's most gifted partner,[21] one of its preeminent choreographers, and eventually Guidi's Associate Artistic Director.

Three years later, Guidi's teaching—this time at Merritt College—attracted another athlete looking for a way to stay in shape during the off-season. Michael Lowe had played three years of varsity football at Alameda's Encinal High as a tailback. "When I got to Merritt," Lowe told reporters at the time, "I wanted to play tennis. So in the off season I took a modern dance class."[22] Lowe's sister, who had once danced for the San Francisco Ballet, suggested that he get stricter with himself and take ballet classes instead. So he did and found that he enjoyed it. Guidi liked Lowe's dancing, with its instinctive grace and supple movement—so much so that he gave him a scholarship to the Oakland Ballet Academy. Since 1973 Michael Lowe has been one of Oakland Ballet's most consistent and lyrical dancers.

Guidi's teaching paid off with more experienced dancers as well. Between the arrival of the two athletes came ballerina Tricia Kaye, who had first studied ballet at the age of eleven. "I had great teachers as a child," Kaye remembers, "such as Gordon Kashman and Willam Christensen, but it wasn't until I came under Ronn's direction that I came into my own as a dancer. He took my body and he made me look like I felt in my mind. He made my lines longer and made me able to really finish my pirouettes and hold my balances."[23]

"Tricia Kaye's arrival was especially important for the inner workings of the Company," recalls Dianne Brock. "In those difficult years, when Ronn Guidi was finding his way from dancing to directing, Tricia was like glue that kept everyone together. . . . As a dancer she was absolutely exquisite, very soft, very lyrical; she could do just about anything."[24]

With a solid group of dancers in hand (to which were soon added Lynne Laakso, John Sullivan, Judy Sandweiss, and Lynn Pendleton), Ronn Guidi returned reinvigorated to the Oakland Ballet and to choreography. Fortified by his experiments with other companies, Guidi faced the new challenges by developing the styles he had already touched upon. There were classical divertissements, such as *Soirée Musicale* and *John Field*

Concerto (both 1971), as well as folk ballets, like *Carnival* (1970), in all of which the emphasis was the unadorned joy of dancing. There were also contemporary pieces that reacted to what was going on in the world, such as *Touch* (1969) and *Apocalypse* (1971), and Tudoresque dance dramas, like *Walk to Paradise Garden* (1970) and *Fragment* (1973).

Walk to Paradise Garden, for example, told the story of two tormented lovers forced to seek in death what life had forbidden them, while *Fragment,* a Victorian period piece, presented an inhibited trio of a pretty girl, a woman who may or may not be her mother, and a handsome, bookish young man, each of whom yearns to break the bonds of convention, but cannot. Sometimes Guidi's scenarios confused individual viewers, as when the combined stories of the Creation, Christ's ministry, passion, and resurrection left Marilyn Tucker of the *San Francisco Chronicle* somewhat mystified after seeing *Fauré Requiem,*[25] but mostly Guidi's new command swept the audience immediately and powerfully into the symbolic world established by each ballet.

As a result of this burst of creative power, seventeen new works by Guidi entered the Oakland Ballet's repertory between 1969 and 1973. Guidi —his confidence in his company restored—was evincing a new mastery, controlling his choreography more tightly, and managing his transitions more fluidly. All that was needed now for the Company to reach its potential was a break into the big league.

The early seventies marked a period of heightened creativity for Ronn Guidi, who gave the Oakland Ballet more than twenty-five works between 1970 and 1975, including "Semiramide" (top left, with Tricia Kaye), "Morning Song" (bottom left, with Dianne Brock and Guidi), "Jupiter" (top right, with David McNaughton and Dianne Brock), and "Landescape" (bottom right, with Tricia Kaye, Robert Warner, and Sally Streets).

A Home Theater,
An Expanded Repertory

In the spring of 1973, Oakland Ballet was still a gypsy caravan—spreading itself out over a variety of locations, such as Merritt College, Oakland's Holy Names High School, Berkeley's Neuman Hall, Hayward's Eden Church, and San Francisco's Golden Gate Park. So long as the Company continued to appear only in churches, high schools, bandshells, and colleges, it would not get the chance of solidly establishing itself either with an audience or with the dance community. Before the Company could take itself seriously —and have others take it seriously—a permanent home in an established theater was needed.

There was a splendid old movie theater in downtown Oakland that had fallen into disrepair and now stood vacant. Built in 1931, the 3,000-seat Paramount was one of those magnificent movie/vaudeville palaces, designed to help transport its audience from the depths of the Depression to the heights of movie magic. Outside, a pair of huge mosaics towered over the front façade, while, inside, golden birds, flowers, and foliage in profusion ornamented an entrance hall of cathedral-like dimensions.

The Oakland Symphony, searching for a new home, was told that it would cost at least $13 million to build a new theater, but only $1 million to purchase the historically irreplaceable Paramount and another $1 million to return it to its former glory. Since the economics of the issue matched the City of Oakland's new sense of itself as a dynamic industrial and cultural center, the Paramount was saved and scheduled to reopen on September 22, 1973.[1] However, the Oakland Symphony, now the owners of the Paramount, did not need the theater full-time. So the managers of the hall began to investigate traveling and local companies interested in the newly renovated facility, which could accommodate opera, ballet, theater, musicals, variety shows, and even movies, as well as symphony concerts.

Looking at the Paramount's yearly schedule, the managers felt in particular that they needed a special holiday show in December, which in modern America meant a production of Tchaikovsky's ballet *The Nutcracker*. The first dance company to bid for the year-end spot was

29

THE LOBBY OF THE PARAMOUNT THEATER

Shortly after the Paramount Theater reopened in 1973, the Oakland Ballet was invited to present a new production of "The Nutcracker." For his version of the Tchaikovsky classic, Guidi returned to E. T. A. Hoffmann's original tale, with its more vivid imagery and more mysterious story-line. Since its 1973 premiere, Guidi's "Nutcracker" has been a showcase for the Company's dancers of all ages, including Patti Owen (below), Howard Sayette (opposite, top), and Cynthia Chin and Ron Thiele (opposite, bottom).

San Francisco Dance Theater. But the management of the Paramount felt an obligation to the East Bay, so they approached the Oakland Ballet. Guidi's company had been performing *Hansel and Gretel* at Christmastime ever since 1963, and the director was loath to follow the common course and substitute *The Nutcracker* for his delicious fairytale ballet. Nevertheless, Guidi was too smart to let this chance slip. So he compromised and pledged the Paramount a *Nutcracker*, if the theater would also book performances of *Hansel and Gretel*.

This arrangement, of course, necessitated a new production of *The Nutcracker*, and if Guidi was going to do it, after having waited so long, he was determined to take the work seriously. Dissatisfied with most of the *Nutcracker*s he had seen, and always conscious of the importance of the dramatic element in ballet, Guidi discarded the watered-down version of the story that Tchaikovsky and Petipa had used for the first production, and turned instead to E. T. A. Hoffmann's original tale, with its more vivid imagery and more mysterious story-line. When Guidi's version premiered as the first ballet at the Paramount on December 19, 1973, it was his concentration on the story that attracted the most attention. Writing in *Dance Magazine*, Pamela Gaye began her catalogue of praise with: "First of all, [Guidi's] characters are real. Once they appear on stage, their presence in the story is felt continually. [Second,] Oakland Ballet's costumes are magical. Wearing yellow empire-period costumes, little girls with long hair-ribbons appeared as flowers. When they dance, it is easy to perceive the dream quality on their six little faces."[2]

The Nutcracker, so long avoided by the Company, became the springboard for its growing success. On the one hand, *The Nutcracker* furnished the Company with an entry into the theater that would soon become its permanent home, and, on the other, it helped the Company cement its relations with the community in which it had lived for nearly ten years. As Guidi commented at the time, "I've recently seen the East Bay go through incredible changes in self-awareness. We are just beginning to find our own personality. An important key in this process, I think, is our ability to tap into the tremendous potential of minority and low-income residents. The Oakland Ballet's *Nutcracker* will be many East Bay children's first contact with ballet, and I want to make it special."[3] Guidi's company already had a long tradition of bringing dance to the children of the Bay Area through lecture-demonstrations, but now the Company, working in conjunction with the City of Oakland and the school districts of Alameda and Contra Costa counties, offered matinees of *The Nutcracker* to local schoolchildren at discount prices. By early November 1973, more than ten thousand such tickets were sold to children and their parents and teachers.

This community outreach was a symbol of Guidi's long-term goal of universalizing dance. Like its surrounding community, Oakland Ballet had developed into a multiracial Company, for (as Guidi wrote to one of his patrons) "we cannot expect minorities to adopt classical ballet unless they can see themselves on stage. I don't believe that a specific body type or a specific race has a monopoly on ballet. We are proud of the variety of our dancers, ranging greatly in temperament, size, emotion and race. We have black, oriental, chicano, and white dancers all jumbled together."[4]

But that was not all. Not only did *The Nutcracker* bring the neighborhoods of East Bay to the Oakland Ballet, it also took the Oakland Ballet out of the East Bay. In fact, the Company had premiered this important new production the year before in Medford, Oregon, on its first major tour. In the weeks before its 1973 Paramount debut, the Company again took *The Nutcracker* on tour, this time a much larger one with twenty-eight performances spread out over Northern California and Oregon. In a little more than two years, a twelve-member subset of the Company, traveling with its own lighting technicians and wardrobe mistress, would visit sixty-seven different cities. By 1975 Oakland had expanded its circuit to include not only California, the Northwest, and British Columbia, but also the American Midwest. Giving three and sometimes four performances out of town to every one in its home theater, Oakland Ballet had become one of the most active touring companies west of the Rockies, even before it received its first National Endowment for the Arts touring grant in 1976. In 1975 alone, a hundred thousand people had seen the Oakland Ballet.[5]

Great as this success was, an incident from 1973 haunted Guidi. That spring saw the Joffrey Ballet's debut in San Francisco's War Memorial Opera House, and before its opening night, Associate Director Gerald Arpino traveled across the bay to see a little-known company called the Oakland Ballet. Arpino was so excited by what he saw that he ventured backstage to congratulate Ronn Guidi not only on his fine dancing of Marc Wilde's *Afternoon of a Faun*, but on his Company as well. After these polite encomiums, Arpino came out with some serious advice. "You are

probably tired of dancing in churches and gymnasiums," he said, "but if you want to get out of this round of little theaters and earn the reputation you deserve, you need to broaden your repertory."[6]

Although Guidi *had* managed to get Oakland Ballet out of that round of churches and gymnasiums, he had to admit to himself that Arpino was right: before he could attract national attention, he would have to establish a strong, more diversified repertory.

Nevertheless, Aprino's proposition pulled Guidi in two directions, for he wanted to continue nurturing Bay Area choreographers. First there was Guidi's own work. Throughout the seventies and despite the Company's ever broadening horizons, Guidi's choreography still represented the single largest group of ballets presented by the Company. In style, Guidi's new work kept to the choreographer's now familiar range. In 1973 there was *Rags*, to the music of Scott Joplin, where the choreography showed off the Company's high spirits and proved that ballet and ragtime could go together. The same year also saw *Blue Danube*, Guidi's tribute to the waltz, and the expansion of *Carmina Burana Pas de Deux* into a full-evening work based on Carl Orff's complete collection of songs. Guidi's *Carmina* represented a particularly pure example of both the choreographer's *joie de vivre* and his continuous search for the dramatic meaning behind movement and music. As Paul Hertelendy in the *Oakland Tribune* explained, "Guidi's dance version follows the original textural threads [of Orff's songs] closely by depicting satyrs in seminarian robes. When their interests turn more seminal than seminarian, they begin peeking into ladies' bodices between pious signs of the cross. Frenzied by the call of love they finally cast off their robes and, in league with a red-wigged devil, cavort about in a bare-chested Walpurgisnacht."[7]

In 1975, when the Company experimented on a grand scale with ballets to commissioned scores, Guidi created the taut, constrained *Landescape* with Bay Area composer Robert Hughes. That same year he created both *Seascape*, an aquatic fantasy with supple, lyrical movement set to the adagio from Aaron Copland's Clarinet Concerto for the Central Valley Ballet, and *Jupiter*, an abstract ballet to Mozart's Symphony No. 41, for his own company.

Guidi's greatest success of the decade, and by common consensus one of his greatest works ever, was *Sibelius* (1978). One would hardly expect Sibelius's mysterious and heroic Fifth Symphony to suit ballet, but it worked because Guidi kept things clean and simple. The movement was purely classical; one critic found it "hinting strongly of Petipa in places,"[8] with a highlight on the ensemble. Lance James, one of Oakland Ballet's most important dancers during these years, remembers the creation of *Sibelius* as especially easy and fluent. "Ronn makes up his movement in the studio, which is fine when everything is flowing smoothly, but when he hits a hard spot, it can take a while to get out of it. With *Sibelius* it was all one rapid stream of inspiration. The ideas just tumbled out of him, which made the rehearsals a particular delight and I think is one of the reasons the work appears so propulsive and seamless. Ronn never had any questions about what he was doing in that one."

Within the Company there was also the emerging voice of Ron Thiele. The young dancer's first venture into choreography, *Brandenburg Concerto No. 2* (1973), immediately showed off his ability to group dancers effectively and to move those groups agilely about the stage, while his second, *Chaconne* (1974), a pas de deux to a score after Vitali, showed, as one critic noted, "outstanding sensitivity of structure. . . . Thiele was not slavish in following the music, but showed a Balanchine-like appreciation for matters of pause and cadence while maintaining a consistency of design and maturity."[9]

Then there was the work of Guidi's old comrade-in-arms, Marc Wilde, who had recently returned in 1972 after an absence of five years. Indeed Wilde's sensuous, Nijinsky-inspired *Afternoon of a Faun*[10] and his clean, rambunctious *Bolero* were among the Company's most frequently performed works during the seventies. In particular, *Bolero* became an integral part of the Company's tours, for its minimal set of an exercise barre and a stepladder was easy to carry around, while its exuberant anything-you-can-do-I-can-do-better spirit made it a surefire hit, "especially," remembers one of the dancers, "in the Midwest, after the movie *Ten* came out."[11]

And there was a newcomer—John Pasqualetti, who had first attracted national fame with his choreography of the rock opera *Tommy*. Pasqualetti's mixture of the risqué and the spiritual fit the ethos of the seventies perfectly. In *Streetcar Named Desire* (1974) the choreographer told a stirring tale of passion, conflict, grief, and insanity—as sultry and Southern as the Tennessee Williams play from which it was derived. In the ballet's twenty minutes, the dancers worked through their intricate relationships and complex emotions with no time to spare. This kind of dramatic

To celebrate the bicentennial in 1976, the Oakland Ballet invited Eugene Loring to stage his Americana master-work, "Billy the Kid." The success of this production began a tradition of historical revivals that was to change the Company's repertory, polish its look, boost its confidence, and enhance its reputation. "Billy the Kid" has since become one of the Company's most highly-regarded works, an important training ground for several of the Company's leading male dancers, including Lance James (opposite, top), David McNaughton (opposite, bottom), and Joral Schmalle (below).

Eugene Loring was so pleased with the Oakland Ballet's production of "Billy the Kid" that he returned to the Company regularly. First there was a revival of his searing drama "The Sisters," in 1977, seen below with Tricia Kaye and Patrice Whiteside. A new work followed the next year, called "The Tender Land," set to a score by Loring's longtime collaborator, Aaron Copland, who traveled to Oakland to conduct the ballet's premiere. Seen here in "The Tender Land" are (opposite, top) Julie Zimmerman-Lowe and Allyson Deane, and (opposite, bottom) Jennifer Young, Patrice Whiteside, Ron Thiele, and Julie Zimmerman-Lowe.

dancing, which took Guidi's own theatrical impulses one step farther, prepared the Company for still more important adventures to come. But it was not in the realm of drama that Pasqualetti made his most lasting contribution to the repertory of the Oakland Ballet; the ballet of his that the Company danced most frequently was *Rite of Spring,* a frenzied celebration of heathen energy that in the end showed how a community can be driven to frightening excesses by ritualized mass hysteria. In addition, *Rite*'s sexual explicitness made it the kind of *succès de scandale* that Guidi appreciated.

Still, the truth behind Arpino's advice lingered in Guidi's mind. He knew that if he was going to gain national attention, he needed to go beyond his own backyard. When Arpino arranged for Oakland to present his *Partita for Four,* he included in the package some of Joffrey's most talented dancers—Christian Holder, Gary Chryst, and Denise Jackson—to spruce up the opening of Guidi's 1974 season with José Limón's *The Moor's Pavane.* In this way, Guidi got the idea of attracting audiences and attention by importing guest artists. For the second 1974 program he added New York City Ballet dancers John Clifford and Sara Leland to the Joffrey quartet, so that Clifford and Leland could dazzle with George Balanchine's *Tarantella* and the Company could perform Clifford's 1969 ballet about ideal love, *Fantasies.*

For the 1975 season Guidi brought in still more outside stars: New York City Ballet dancer Kyra Nichols, who was the daughter of Oakland Ballet dancer Sally Streets; a Swedish couple, Walter Bourke and Maria Lange, who danced Bourke's *Romeo and Juliet Pas de Deux;* and American Ballet Theatre's black star, Keith Lee. While Kyra Nichols joined Ron Thiele for a smoldering rendition of Wilde's *Afternoon of a Faun,* Bourke set his *Grand Tarantella* on Oakland's fastest rising star, David McNaughton, partnered by the Company's classicist, Janet Carole. In addition to dancing, Lee set two of his own works, *Us* and *Times Past,* on the Company as well.

While these guest stars certainly helped bring a new audience to the Oakland Ballet, they could not lift the Company into the realm Guidi wanted for it. Like children circling the perimeter of a traveling circus because they did not have the admission price, the Company was now dancing around the national arena. They could see in, they had even attracted the attention of some of the circus denizens, but they were still shut out from the excitement.

Then Guidi, searching for a special bicentennial ballet for the 1976 season, hit upon the solution: he invited Eugene Loring to stage his most famous work, *Billy the Kid,* on the Oakland Ballet. With his interest in dramatic ballets that pushed dancers beyond technique, Loring was uniquely placed to appreciate Oakland Ballet's sometimes unpolished strengths. Of course, a host of other companies, including the San Francisco Ballet, wanted Loring that year. When the 62-year-old choreographer chose the Oakland Ballet instead of some more prominent companies, it turned the eyes of dance professionals westward. When Loring declared Oakland Ballet's version of *Billy the Kid* the definitive one, the circus gate was suddenly opened.

Jack Anderson of the *New York Times* later explained exactly why Oakland Ballet's production of *Billy* attracted and rewarded so much interest. "*Billy the Kid* received a scrupulously coached revival by the choreographer," wrote Anderson. "Patterns were clear and gestures detailed, yet the production never appeared finicky. The dancers in the complex contrapuntal ensembles were not merely figures in a design, but also recognizable members of a frontier community. And all poses and movements possessed dramatic significance. For instance, when someone put a hand in front of his face, one realized that he had gone into hiding. A hand held stiffly at a slight distance from the body became a hand of cards. And when someone tossed an invisible card, one knew from the strength of the gesture and the reaction of other characters just how high it was tossed and where it fell."[12]

Loring himself was so pleased with the Company's rendition of *Billy the Kid* that he returned to the Company each season for the next three years. Indeed, until a brain tumor began to incapacitate him, the choreographer faithfully gave the Company not only his ballets, but his creative genius and his expert eye as well. First there was a revival of *The Sisters* in 1977, a searing melodrama so potent that one of Oakland Ballet's dancers told Loring she simply could not perform it.[13] A new work followed, called *The Tender Land* (1978), set to the orchestral suite from an opera of the same name by Loring's old collaborator Aaron Copland. To commemorate this reunion, Copland himself traveled to Oakland to conduct the work's premiere together with a revival of *Billy the Kid* and Guidi's *Seascape.* Loring's last ballet, a plotless meditation on man's inhumanity to man, *Time Unto Time* (1980), was also his last gift to the thriving Oakland

company that he himself had done so much to bolster.

Loring's importance to the Oakland Ballet was greater than the outside interest he focused on the Company. Something happened during Loring's visits to the dancers themselves. Patrice Whiteside, who had studied with Loring at the University of California, Irvine, before joining the Oakland Ballet, and who would later become the artistic executor of Loring's estate, remembers that "working with Loring was really different for Ronn and the dancers. Loring was extremely meticulous and exacting. Where someone like Pasqualetti would come in and create on the spot, allowing the dancers to integrate their own thoughts into the choreography, Loring knew exactly what he wanted and how to go about it. . . . [With *Billy the Kid*] Ronn gave Loring total control, in terms of casting, hours, everything, which delighted Loring because he had just come out of a bad experience with [American] Ballet Theatre. Working with Loring gave Ronn and the dancers more than just a new prestige, it gave them a new sense of the possibilities of dance."

Besides whipping the dancers into a physical shape and insisting on a level of concentration they had never known before, Loring also confirmed the Company's interest in dramatic ballet.[14] As Whiteside sums it up, "Loring was always telling me that there was no movement happening without an emotion behind it." That was the truth that Loring took with him to the Oakland Ballet and the one he left in the Company's keeping.

Finding another choreographer who could further enrich both the Company and its repertory as Loring had done, set Guidi on a difficult search. Then, by chance, he heard that Léonide Massine was in the Bay Area instructing the Marin Ballet—Massine, one of the century's greatest dancers and the choreographer Serge Diaghilev had hand-picked to succeed Nijinsky. Guidi coaxed the now elderly artist over to see the Oakland dancers. When the master declared himself pleased with what he saw, Guidi encouraged Massine to return to set *La Boutique Fantasque*, his 1919 fantasy of a revolt by the toys in a specialty shop.

Working with Massine could not be for the Oakland Ballet the experience that working with Loring had been, because by 1978 Massine was elderly and his body ravaged. His rehearsals were labored; he had forgotten much of *La Boutique*'s choreography, and had to be reminded of it by his assistant. Nevertheless the experience did provide the Oakland dancers with unique insights into the world of Diaghilev's Ballets Russes.

Massine brought with him stories from long ago and a way of thinking full of mystery and charm for the young, energetic American dancers. He also brought a telling instrument of instruction. His own body was so thoroughly trained and so completely inspired by dance that even though he could no longer walk with ease, Massine would magically become supple and agile whenever he chose to demonstrate a movement. It was this transformation that struck awe in the dancers and taught them what it was like to love dancing so much that in its service one could overcome almost any physical obstacle.

As he would continue to do with all his Diaghilev revivals, Guidi sought to bring not only Massine's amusing comedy back to life, but the stage-world in which it had been first presented as well. Part and parcel of all Diaghilev ballets were their sets and costumes, with designs frequently commissioned from the finest painters alive. André Derain, one of the painters who together with Matisse and Rouault formed the group known as the Fauves, created the decor for *La Boutique Fantasque*. When famed British art historian Roger Fry specifically reviewed Derain's contribution to the ballet, he pointed both to its "purest French classicism . . . [the] precise accent of high civilization," and its "uproarious fun . . . [a] subversion of all standards of verisimilitude."[15] Oakland Ballet lovingly copied Derain's backdrop and show-curtain, thereby establishing a pattern for revivals that would verify the Company's integrity in all aspects of its work. When Massine saw the premiere of Oakland's version of *La Boutique* on October 27, 1978, he told Guidi, "You have made the spirit of Diaghilev live again."

Such bounding success had, of course, changed the Oakland Ballet. On March 25, 1974, the Company had taken a giant step into its own future and organized a seven-member Board of Directors, headed by Company director Ronn Guidi together with president Michael A. Lawson, and including such arts patrons as Marcia Fogel, Arthur M. Choy, Cecile Keaveney, Dr. Harold B. Swaner, and Richard D. King.[16] The formation of a Board represented a crucial step in the institutionalization of the Company. It provided the Oakland Ballet with an experienced, worldly group that could deal with large-scale funding sources both in governmental agencies and in the business community.

Yet some aspects of the grass-roots community organization remained. The same spring that saw Oakland Ballet's first Board formed saw everyone rolling up their sleeves and pitching in to convert an old laundromat into a

One of the Oakland Ballet's leading contemporary choreographers during the seventies was John Pasqualetti, whose mixture of the risqué and the spiritual fit the ethos of the decade perfectly. Pasqualetti gave the Company five works between 1974 and 1978, including a stirring version of "A Streetcar Named Desire" (below, with Tricia Kaye and Ron Thiele), a dramatic "Resurrection" (opposite, bottom), and a sexually provocative production of "The Rite of Spring" (opposite, top with Susan Taylor and Ron Thiele).

new studio. The dancers became a construction crew, Ron Thiele laid the floor, and those Board members stood shoulder to shoulder with the young dancers to help paint the new facility. In its first twenty-five years Oakland Ballet would never lose its home-town, we're-all-in-it-together atmosphere, but in the early and mid-seventies it was also becoming a fully-formed artistic institution with a firm administrative structure and an active fund-raising Board.

The Company had begun the decade as a chamber group, made up primarily of youngsters living at home, spiced by a few diehard adults able to work for almost nothing. In 1972 the Oakland Ballet had eight dancers, presenting sixteen in-school performances, forty-eight lecture-demonstrations (divided evenly between those for children and those for the general public), sixteen master-classes and sixty-eight performances. Their total audience was not more than eighteen thousand.

With the help of governmental grants administered through CETA, the Company had grown by 1975 to thirty-six dancers, seen by more than a hundred thousand people. In addition, money came in from the City of Oakland ($3,500) and the County of Alameda ($5,000). By 1976 the Company had edged its way into the select group favored by the National Endowment for the Arts. The Company's first NEA production grant was a matching one for *Billy the Kid* in the amount of $9,320; its first touring grant came in 1976 as well. The touring grant was doubly important because in those years the NEA picked up one-third of a sponsor's cost for any NEA touring company, an arrangement that made such groups most attractive to booking agents.

With rising contributions came also rising costs: in 1976 the price for just one day at the Paramount Theater was $3,000 and the cost for the *Nutcracker* orchestra alone was $22,000. When those 1976 *Nutcracker* receipts were totaled, the Company had made $27,500. It gave back $12,000 to those Board members who had made loans out of their own pockets, kept $5,000 for operating expenses, and paid $11,000 to eager creditors clamoring for more.

The total year's budget for 1975–76 was $191,000, up from something like $10,000 in 1970. For the next five years, the growth rate was steady: $321,000 for 1976–77, $508,000 for 1977–78, $617,000 for 1978–79, and $744,000 for 1979–80. In that last season, earned income amounted to $411,200—$231,200 of which came from touring and $128,273 from *The*

Nutcracker. Some $310,000 was amassed by contributed income, of which the biggest portion was CETA money amounting to $125,000, followed by corporation and foundation donations of $95,000. All that still left a deficit of $20,000, adding to an ever-expanding problem.[17]

Oakland Ballet had grown enormously in the seventies both in artistic quality and financial resources. But its very success ironically made it more precarious than ever. As many arts administrators have noted, the more successful you are, the greater is your deficit. In 1975, at the same time that the San Francisco Ballet was fighting for its life with an S.O.B. (Save Our Ballet) campaign, the Oakland company was launching one of its own, called Save An Endangered Species. In 1975 the Company had to cancel its spring season for lack of money; in 1979 it again had to do the same thing. Success had not ruined the Oakland Ballet—nor, for the moment, had it given it stability.

In 1978 the legendary Diaghilev dancer-choreographer Léonide Massine (opposite, top) came to Oakland to stage his 1919 ballet "La Boutique Fantasque," which featured such whimsical characters as dancing poodles (opposite, below) and can-can dolls (below, with Mario Alonzo and Erin Leedom). Massine provided the Oakland dancers with unique insights into the world of Diaghilev's Ballets Russes, and began a series of distinguished Diaghilev revivals. Today, the Oakland Ballet has one of the most important Diaghilev repertoires in the country.

The Nijinska Ballets and International Recognition

In 1976, *Billy the Kid* had begun a tradition of historical revivals that was to change the Company's repertory, polish its look, boost its confidence, and enhance its reputation. That same year the famed Diaghilev dancer Anatole Vilzak staged Michel Fokine's *Le Spectre de la Rose* for Oakland dancers David McNaughton and Janet Carole. These works established the two facets of Guidi's exploration into the past: the American side that recalled the best and most characteristic accomplishments of our culture, and the Diaghilev side that sought to revivify the fabled world of the great Russian impresario. Following this auspicious beginning came, in quick succession, Oakland's new production of *Coppélia* in 1977 (based on Nicholas Sergeyev's 1933 staging for the Vic-Wells Ballet), both Massine's *La Boutique Fantasque* and Eugene Loring's *The Sisters* in 1978; Fokine's *Sheherazade*, with its exquisitely wrought decors after Léon Bakst's original, and Massine's *Le Soleil de Nuit* in 1979; and, beginning the new decade, Anna Sokolow's *Rooms*.

As a symbol of the Oakland Ballet's new place in the dance world, the Company embarked on two major tours in 1981: the first took the dancers to New York's Brooklyn College in the spring, while the second flew them for three weeks to France and Italy in the summer. For the New York appearances two programs were assembled, showing that in the midst of all these heady revivals, the Company had not forgotten its commitment to the present. Revivals of *Billy* and *Sheherazade* were seen as contrasts to the work of several contemporary California choreographers, including Marc Wilde's saucy *Bolero*, John Pasqualetti's rambunctious *Rite of Spring*, Eugene Loring's probing *Time unto Time*, and two of Ronn Guidi's own latest delights, the commedia dell'arte romp *Carnival d'Aix* and the insouciant *Gallops and Kisses*, together with the old standby *Trois Gymnopédies*.

The European tour began in Nice, proceeded to Genoa for the Nervi Festival, then continued to Turin, Modena, and Naples with all performances in the open air. For this excursion the Company took a full

LANCE JAMES AND ERIN LEEDOM IN
BRONISLAVA NIJINSKA'S *LES BICHES*

In 1981 the Oakland Ballet became the first American company to present Bronislava Nijinska's legendary but rarely-performed ballet "Les Noces." The Company's production of this Diaghilev-era masterpiece swept the country's dance community into a state of wonderment, bringing the Company its first flush of international recognition. "It is not simply that the Oakland Ballet has reproduced an innovative and once controversial work with care and historical accuracy," said Walter Terry. "To the contrary, the Company dances it as if it were new." Seen here are various of the ballet's distinctive moments, with Summer Lee Rhatigan as the Bride (opposite, top).

Copland evening, featuring Loring's *Billy*, as well as Guidi's *Seascape* and *El Salón México*. Other programs included both Wilde's *Afternoon of a Faun* and *Bolero*, and a string of Guidi's recent works, including *Carnival d'Aix*, *Gallops and Kisses*, *Sibelius*, and *In Autumn*.

With fame now catching up to the Oakland Ballet, the Company prepared for its greatest triumph to date. Back in 1978 Léonide Massine had suggested that if the Company wanted to increase its Diaghilev repertory it should seek out Bronislava Nijniska's daughter, who was living in California, and ask permission to remount her mother's ballets. In 1981, through the agency of *Dance Magazine* editor William Como, Guidi contacted Irina Nijinska and invited her in the late summer to oversee the first American production of Nijinska's world-famous but rarely performed *Les Noces*.[1]

Oakland Ballet's *Les Noces* swept the country's dance community into a state of wonderment. In the *San Francisco Examiner* the day after its September 25, 1981 premiere, Allan Ulrich called the production "an historic occasion." Highlighting the care Oakland had taken with the sets and costumes as well with the ballet itself, Ulrich proclaimed: "*Les Noces* has been meticulously and tenderly recreated. . . . Natalia Gontcharova's stark brown and white costumes were duplicated with love, and Robert Klemm's lighting helped to intensify this eternal rite of passage. But the bouquets must finally go to the thirty-six performers. The intensity of their work, their grasp of Stravinsky's subtle rhythmic scheme and the immaculate discipline of their ensemble marked this as dancing of international caliber."[2]

Nor was it only the local press that rejoiced in Oakland Ballet's accomplishment. Walter Terry, the dean of American dance critics, writing of the Company's appearance at the Spoleto Festival U.S.A, exclaimed: "To see the Oakland Ballet dance Bronislava Nijinska's *Les Noces* is an enthralling, bewitching, riveting experience. . . . I recall the Ballet Russe de Monte Carlo restaging many years ago without much pleasure, and the more recent revival by Britain's Royal Ballet with great disappointment. Jerome Robbins's wholly new version made many of us think that Nijinska's original was obsolete. But no more. The Oakland Ballet has resurrected a masterwork of the Diaghilev era. . . . It is not simply that the Oakland Ballet has reproduced an innovative and once controversial work with care and historical accuracy. To the contrary, the Company dances it as if it were new, as if the dancers were relishing its primitive energies for the first time. . . . The company itself is neither as large or as technically polished as the Royal Ballet, but its very crudities are assets in this production."[3] Irina Nijinska, the choreographer's daughter, who had come to Oakland to oversee the new production, said the same thing but more succinctly: "I knew they would dance it well. A company that strives only for classical perfection lacks the heavy character movement needed for Diaghilev ballets."[4]

The success of *Les Noces* in 1981 was followed the next year by the same choreographer's *Les Biches*, as light and witty as *Les Noces* was severe and serious. The Nijinska ballets not only proclaimed the Oakland Ballet as Nijinska's central American advocate, but reaffirmed it as one of the nation's primary caretakers of the Diaghilev repertory. During the same year as it presented *Les Biches*, for example, the Company also premiered Fokine's *Polovetsian Dances* (1909), as staged by the distinguished Ballet Russe dancer Frederic Franklin, who, in 1987, would also set the Company's first *Giselle*. "Freddie came from a ballet culture that had a very literary view of art, one that Ronn Guidi shares," recalls Associate Director Ron Thiele. "When we finished with *Giselle*, we knew that ballet in and out as dancers and as human beings."[5]

The year 1983 brought the Company its first Agnes de Mille ballet, *Inconsequentials*. Back in 1976, when Guidi first approached de Mille, her response was a terse, "Who's the Oakland Ballet?" Now she explained to Guidi, "My spies tell me you have a very good company."[6] *Inconsequentials*, a light trifle, taught the Company more about a style than about content. Oakland's second de Mille ballet, *Fall River Legend*, on the other hand, emphasized the Company's almost Dostoevskian sense of drama. Together with *The Green Table*, which entered the repertory in 1984, two years before *Fall River*, this succinct and haunting tale of Lizzie Borden's ax showed the mid-eighties Oakland Ballet at its striking best. In the same vein, and showing the Company off equally well, was Charles Weidman's *Lynchtown* (1985), the most concentrated of these psychological investigations into the frighteningly violent nature of the human animal.

These three dance-dramas, together with *Giselle* in its very different and romantic way, prepared Oakland for Antony Tudor's *Lilac Garden* in 1989. "Tudor was so notorious in the dance world for his biting criticisms," explains Ron Thiele, "that we were all wondering what working with

Tudor's hand-picked executor would be like. But Sallie Wilson, to our surprise, turned out to be a caring, generous person. *Lilac Garden* is, of course, a ballet of a thousand details, and Sallie focused keenly on each one. Nothing escaped her watchful eye, but she did it all in such a loving way that those sessions, though strenuous, were a delight."[7] *Lilac Garden* began a collaboration that will continue into Oakland's next twenty-five years. Tudor's *Echoing of Trumpets*, which he choreographed for the Royal Swedish Ballet in 1963 and which has rarely been seen in America, will appear in the 1991 season, while *Dark Elegies* is scheduled for 1992.

Crowning this decade—and ending it almost as it began—was the Oakland Ballet's lavish 1989 reconstruction of Bronislava Nijinska's *Le Train Bleu*. This ballet, last seen in 1924, was long thought suitable only for dust-gathering history books, but Oakland Ballet brought it back to life through the efforts of dance scholar Frank W. D. Ries. Aided by the expertise on every aspect of her mother's choreography possessed by Irina Nijinska, Ries was able to revivify not only Nijinska's steps, but also Chanel's elegantly amusing costumes and Picasso's impressive drop curtain, though recovering Laurens's chic sets did give the Company some difficulty.

For the premiere of this production, dance critics and enthusiasts assembled from the four corners of the country—and beyond. Though a critic like Tobi Tobias (perhaps looking for a more serious drama than she found) called the Oakland dancers "generally deficient in clarity, weight and individuality,"[8] most agreed with Jack Anderson of the *New York Times*, when he admitted, "Sometimes a work is worth preserving simply because it is fun. The Oakland Ballet deserves praise for reviving *Le Train Bleu*, the bathing-beach romp choreographed by Bronislava Nijinska."[9] Janice Ross of *Dance Magazine*, impressed by the "theatrical vitality" of this reconstruction, understood that it was a work dependent not on bravura but on that ineffable quality, style. "The characters of the four key figures," Ross wrote, "—the Tennis Champion (wonderfully danced by the sultry Susan Taylor), Perlouse (the bathing beauty, dryly done by Abra Rudisill), the Beau Gosse (the robust and boyish Michael Lowe in his best role in years), and the Golfer (a low-keyed Ron Thiele)—were conveyed as much through nuances . . . as steps."[10]

The glory of these revivals and the reason they have constituted such an important training vehicle for the Company is that Oakland Ballet does not just put on *Les Noces* or *Sheherazade*, *Billy the Kid* or *The Green Table*,

Lynchtown or *Les Biches* for a season or two and then let it drop. Guidi brings them back constantly, giving the performers the chance to work on these masterpieces repeatedly, and in the process to live with their greatness until it seeps into their minds, their bodies, and their souls.

But despite its emphasis on historic revivals, Oakland Ballet is not a museum. From the mid-seventies when Guidi devised his plan of revivals, they constituted only one side of his policy "to preserve and create history." Throughout the eighties, while it gained fame from its revivals, Oakland Ballet also served as a living instrument for contemporary choreographers, and in particular Bay Area artists.

Within the Company, Ron Thiele continued to choreograph on a steady basis. Two important breakthroughs for Thiele came with *Amis* in 1982 and then again with *How'd They Catch Me?* in 1989. "Freed for the first time from his mentor Ronn Guidi's movement strings," wrote Marilyn Tucker of the *San Francisco Chronicle*, Thiele "particularly impressed" with his "rocklike musicality [in *Amis*]. There wasn't a soft moment. Each sequence depended on what had gone before and gave life to what was to come."[11] In *How'd They Catch Me?* Thiele once again found a new burst of creative energy, or, as Ronn Guidi has said, "He found a new voice, witty, almost casual, but profound."[12]

Perhaps the most intriguing new choreographic talent that Guidi has brought to the fore in the eighties is that of Oakland's ballet mistress, Betsy Erickson. A dancer of impeccable precision and classic self-restraint, Erickson has become a many-faceted choreographer whose work ranges from the exotically textured mixture of classical and modern dancing seen in *Waterways* to the light, bright, but technically challenging *Sfumato*, her tribute to mentor Lew Christensen.

But Oakland Ballet's contemporary repertory is not merely a vehicle for its own staff; it is open to many other talents from several different Bay Area companies. In 1983, for example, San Francisco–based Carlos Carvajal, who had worked with the Company in the early and mid-seventies, returned to oversee the setting of his full-length Cinderella ballet, *The Crystal Slipper*, premiered by Dance Spectrum five years earlier. In 1984 he returned again, this time to create *Synergies*, an exploration into what Carvajal called "the angularity, harshness and longing so prevalent in today's society."[13] During this same time, the National Choreography Project singled out the Oakland Ballet as the only West Coast company to receive a

During the past 15 years, the Oakland Ballet has assembled an impressive body of American masterworks, works that, with great flair and imagination, capture the spirit of this country and its diverse peoples. The Company's American "wing" includes such noted works as Agnes de Mille's "Fall River Legend" (opposite, top with Summer Lee Rhatigan and Ron Thiele), Anna Sokolow's powerful "Rooms" (opposite, bottom with Michael Lowe), and Ruthanna Boris's delightful period piece, "Cakewalk" (below, with Brad Bradley).

45

grant encouraging modern dance choreographers to work with classically trained ballet companies. As a result Santa Cruz's Tandy Beal traveled north to create . . . *this harsh spectacle, this invisible activity, this sense* . . . in 1984, and San Francisco's Brenda Way crossed the Bay to collaborate with artist Wayne Theibaud on *This Point in Time* in 1987. San Francisco Ballet dancer/choreographer Val Caniparoli contributed three works to Oakland's repertory in the eighties, while Emily Keeler created a startling mediation on Kate Chopin's novel *The Awakening* in 1988.

The pressures of running this ambitious and thriving company, however, cut substantially into Ronn Guidi's own choreographic output. After a burst of activity that included *Carnival d'Aix, Ballade,* and *In Autumn* in 1980, *Fantasia para un Gentilhombre* in 1981, and *Dvorak Dances* in 1982, Guidi produced only the unfinished *Nicholas and Concepcion* in 1987. But Guidi is not depressed by this turn of events. "It is the Company that is important to me," he says. "I choreograph when I can for the Company, and so long as they are thriving, I am satisfied."[14]

Within little more than a decade, Guidi had, in fact, assembled one of the most satisfying and diverse repertories in the nation—a repertoire that was markedly different from that of the Company's larger and better-known neighbor across the bay, the San Francisco Ballet. (San Francisco Ballet under Lew Christensen had been for years a Balanchine-influenced company, and even after Michael Smuin joined Christensen as company-director in 1973, the company's repertoire continued in the same vein, spiced by Smuin's more spectacular productions.) In 1983, the Oakland Ballet—wanting to redefine its position in the marketplace so as to emphasize its repertorial difference in a more vivid way for the audience—began presenting its home season during the fall, taking it out of "competition" with the San Francisco Ballet, which performed during the winter and spring. As a result, Oakland Ballet had a 370 percent increase in subscription sales.

The distinguished expansion of Oakland Ballet's repertoire did not, however, come without its price: a budget that had increased from $191,000 for 1975–76, the year before *Billy the Kid*, to $1.2 million for 1981–82, the year of *Les Noces.*

Like all artistic organizations in the United States, Oakland suffered throughout the eighties from the withering of governmental support. First there was the dismantling of CETA, which had been a perfect program for the Oakland Ballet because it was designed to help disadvantaged youth train for jobs they could otherwise never have dreamed of. In 1980 government support of the Oakland Ballet accounted for 50 percent of its annual contributions; by 1982 that percentage had dropped to 25 percent.[15]

With the decrease in income came, paradoxically, the usual increase in expenses. By 1983, the Company was offering twenty dancers at least $1,000 a month with a ten-month guarantee.[16] The cost of auditorium rentals and new production budgets rose likewise. By December 31, 1983, the Company's audit showed an accumulated deficit of $163,500.[17] By 1984–85, budget projections foretold a deficit of $348,700.[18] In only a couple of years, this very kind of deficit financing would bankrupt the Oakland Symphony.

The Oakland Ballet was able to weather the storm, partly because of the alertness of its general manager, Mark Denton; partly by the readiness of its community-oriented Board of Directors, headed by Lois DeDomenico at the turn of the decade and later by Ian Zellick, Frank Spiller, William P. Barlow, Jr., Mrs. John Bonham, Fred Karren, and Roger D. Hardy; and certainly because of the willingness of all involved to pitch in and help. The dancers and administrative staff, for example, took a temporary 10-percent cut in pay in 1984–85, while the Board members gave increased amounts out of their own pockets, and where they could not afford to give outright they made loans to the struggling Company. Guidi had always been willing to substitute recordings for live music in a performance, and now he put off some long cherished projects as well. But these were only patchwork answers to meet immediate demands.

As a solution to its budgetary crisis, the Company launched an intensive twentieth anniversary campaign aimed at raising a total of $2 million in contributed income. This funding drive began with a $30,000 donation from Mervyn's/Dayton Hudson Foundation in August 1985 and continued for three years, until the Company was able to retire its debt entirely and to secure additional working capital for special projects like new choreography, live music, and increased dancers' salaries. To further stabilize the Company's finances, another major fundraising effort was launched in 1990, in conjunction with the Company's silver anniversary. This new effort—called Campaign 2000—aims to raise $3.7 million in three years: $1.5 million for production enhancement, wider community access, and increased financial stability, and $2.2 million for ongoing program support.

Throughout the late seventies and eighties, the Oakland Ballet faced an issue that many midsize companies encounter: the loss of its dancers to larger organizations. David McNaughton, the Company's brightest light in the mid-seventies and its first Billy, had long ago gone off to San Francisco Ballet, from which he would later move to the New York City Ballet. Likewise, Jim Sohm had departed for San Francisco Ballet, while the engaging David Roland had flown off to the Deutsche Oper Ballet in Berlin. In the spring of 1983 Lance James broke his knee coming down from Billy the Kid's double tour, a movement he had performed over three hundred times. So he went from having the spotlight shined on him to calling the spotlight cues as the Company's production stage manager.

To fill the void caused by these multiple departures, several of the Company's own younger dancers now moved into the front ranks. Julie Lowe, trained by Guidi at the Oakland Ballet Academy before joining the Company in 1974, had grown into a pure yet imaginative dancer, best in dramatic parts like Gretel in *Hansel and Gretel*, Maria in *The Nutcracker*, and Giselle, where one could see a real character shining through the warm and generous performer. Shirlee Reevie, a large, graceful dancer who had been with the Eliot Feld Ballet before coming to the Oakland Ballet in 1977, developed into a dancer who could dazzle with her beautiful feet and an exciting jump. Susan Taylor would emerge by the end of the eighties as a truly gifted comedienne, with her long legs and deadpan face. She was particularly striking in May O'Donnell's *Pursuit of Happiness* and Ruthanna Boris's *Cakewalk*, but most especially in Nijinska's own role of the tennis player in *Le Train Bleu*. Mario Alonzo, who like Taylor had joined Oakland from the Central Valley Dance Company, would come to shine in quick, athletic parts like the Can-Can Doll in Massine's *La Boutique Fantasque* and the Jester in Carlos Carvajal's *The Crystal Slipper*, as well as an ebullient Peter in Ronn Guidi's 1990 edition of *Peter and the Wolf*.

Among the dancers who had joined Oakland Ballet in the late seventies, however, one in particular stood out. When Guidi first worked with Erin Leedom in 1976 at the Central Valley Dance Company, he was immediately struck by this "blonde and beautiful, yet simple dancer."[19] Leedom's simplicity, which shone through a fine technique, encouraged her to maintain a wonderfully unselfconscious approach to dancing. When Ruthanna Boris set *Cakewalk* on Oakland Ballet in 1983, she observed that "Erin has a way of becoming her role." When *Les Biches* confirmed the

Company's role as the American advocate of Nijinska's choreography in 1982, Leedom, as the mysterious Girl in Blue, was likewise catapulted to fame. With finely chiseled features, but a bright, stage-filling energy, Leedom would later become the Company's first and most delicate Giselle.

Complementing these rising stars from within were others Guidi imported from without. Among the most compelling was Summer Lee Rhatigan, who had trained at the Royal Ballet School in London and danced with the London Festival Ballet before joining Oakland Ballet in 1983. Rhatigan was an explosive dancer who reached her greatest height as the Lizzie Borden figure in Agnes de Mille's *Fall River Legend*. In that work she gave what Paul Parish in *Ballet Review* called "a performance beyond praise. . . . Rhatigan is a strong, earthy dancer with . . . a technique that does anything she needs it to. Her face was unforgettable, a tragic mask peering out from the crowd [gathered] around the scaffold, or jerking desperately in all directions above a floating, arabesque turn."[20]

In the mid-eighties, the Company's male contingent was bolstered by the arrival of two very different dancers: the fifteen-year-old Joral Schmalle, whom the *Oakland Tribune* noted in his 1983 debut season as being "among the singularly impressive dancers,"[21] and Don Schwennesen,

In 1984 the Oakland Ballet presented a distinguished revival of Kurt Jooss's 1932 antiwar masterpiece, "The Green Table" (below). Among the ballet's most arresting figures is that of Death, danced by one of the Oakland Ballet's most versatile performers, Ron Thiele (opposite, top and bottom).

an already established dancer who came to Oakland with his wife, Allyson Deanne, from San Francisco Ballet in 1984.

When the Oakland Ballet returned to New York in 1985, *The New York Times* noticed the new dancers. "There are new, better dancers," wrote Anna Kisselgoff, "and improved dancers with a stronger and more classical technique. Moreover, while one could sympathize in [Oakland's] initial visit with Guidi's rare openness to a disparity of body types, the company seemed to be making more of a social statement than a firm artistic one. The differences are still evident. But now they are incidental, with the dancers impressing themselves upon the eye on purely artistic grounds. Perhaps this is because they are used primarily as dancers—a result of the change toward a repertory with a stronger artistic profile."[22]

Helping the Company on this road to renewal were its three ballet masters, Ronn Guidi, Howard Sayette, and Betsy Erickson. Sayette, who had danced with the Ballet Russe de Monte Carlo in the fifties and the Metropolitan Opera Ballet in the sixties, had learned a dramatic, pre-Balanchine way of thinking about ballet from his work with Alexandra Danilova, Alicia Markova, Bronislava Nijinska, and Katherine Dunham. Since becoming a permanent member of the artistic staff in 1978, Sayette had symbolized his link with this past by taking over several dramatic roles, such as the Shah in *Sheherazade*, the Shopkeeper in *La Boutique Fantasque*, and the Father in *Crystal Slipper.* Erickson, Oakland's ballet mistress since 1984, brought with her a dramatic background from her training with Raoul Pausé and her time with the American Ballet Theater (1967–72), as well as a Balanchine-like fondness for the abstract from her training with Lew Christensen and her work both before and after ABT with the San Francisco Ballet.

Even a unique repertory, skilled ballet masters, and a strong esprit de corps, however, cannot stem the passage of time. By the end of the decade, the Company that so impressed Kisselgoff in 1985 had begun to change. As the older dancers aged, they either retired or adapted to new roles. Meanwhile several of the younger ones followed the call of their expanding careers. Though he continued to dance, partnering with his customary grace and charm, Ron Thiele, for example, was now more impressive in character roles, such as his masterful performance of Death in *The Green Table.* Thiele's major contribution to the Company in the last half of the decade was, in fact, not as a dancer, but as Guidi's Associate Artistic

Director and as one of its most interesting choreographers. Throughout the decade Mario Alonzo had honed his skills as costume designer and builder as well as dancer; for the twenty-fifth anniversary season he would develop yet another skill by choreographing his first ballet. By the end of the decade, even the athletic Michael Lowe, one of the Company's most dependable and consistently rewarding dancers, was beginning to show the effects of his seventeen years with the Company. Among the women, Erin Leedom left for Ballet West in 1987, Summer Lee Rhatigan for the National Ballet of Canada in 1989, and Susan Taylor for the Vienna production of *Cats* in 1990. Julie Lowe, who had danced her whole career with the Oakland Ballet, turned in her toe shoes in 1990.

Once again Guidi looked first within his own company for the needed renewal. The sparrow-like Abra Rudisill had grown tremendously since joining the Company in 1982. Naturally a soubrette, Rudisill disciplined herself to the classics, becoming in time a lovely Giselle, whose beautiful, sylph-like jumps made Act II especially thrilling. Rudisill's nervously intense work in *Lynchtown* fit Weidman's violent drama perfectly, while her work in Emily Keeler's *The Awakening* showed a maturing histrionic range.

This void at the top has brought forward two other homegrown talents. Both Joy Gim and Cynthia Chin came up through the Oakland Ballet Academy, had been apprentices with the Company, and in the last years of the eighties were becoming ballerinas in their own right. The turning point for Gim was her first Sugarplum Fairy—for one must remember that in this Company, despite its international repertory, *The Nutcracker* has always remained the touchstone of classical purity. What was remarkable about Gim's first Sugarplum, observed Ron Thiele, was the way it was so carefully thought through. It proclaimed that here was a determined, fully conscious ballerina on her way toward a notable career. Unlike Gim, who had to work for her greatness, Chin was one of those natural dancers whose technique seems boundless. She showed her gifts early; her teachers' role was more to reveal them than to create them. As with Leedom, Chin has used the mysterious Girl in Blue in *Les Biches* as a vehicle to move from an adolescent innocence to an ambiguous sophistication.

Like Gim and Chin, the Oakland Ballet, entering its twenty-fifth year with the 1990 fall season, is in the process of maturation. Now, however, it is fortified by what is one of the most broadly ranging repertories in the country. It has works from the classical period of ballet to teach smoothness of technique, line, and grace. It has many Diaghilev-era ballets to steep the dancers in the history of modern art. It has great American works to bring the dancers back to their own cultural roots. And it has a thrilling contemporary repertory that speaks to the world the dancers see around them. It is a repertory that can attract, train, and—most importantly—satisfy Oakland's dancers of tomorrow.

In twenty-five years, Ronn Guidi has created a school, a company, and a repertory that is the embodiment of this country's great thirst for movement, grace, music, history, and excitement. In this way, the Oakland Ballet is one of our truest examples of the fabulous dance boom that has brought art and beauty into the lives of so many Americans.

Crowning the Company's first twenty-five years was its lavish 1989 reconstruction of Bronislava Nijinska's "Le Train Bleu," with drop curtain by Pablo Picasso, costumes by Coco Chanel, and libretto by Jean Cocteau. This Diaghilev ballet, last seen in 1924, was long thought suitable only for dust-gathering history books, but Oakland Ballet brought it back to life. The ballet is a witty portrait of the twenties, complete with such contemporary characters as a golfer (Don Schwennesen), a tennis player (Susan Taylor), and young bathers at a beach (Abra Rudisill and Michael Lowe, opposite). "Le Train Bleu" marked the third Nijinska ballet staged by the Oakland Ballet, which has thus become the principal American advocate of the Nijinska legacy.

The Company's Repertory: A Directory

COMPILED BY WILLIAM HUCK

The following directory lists those ballets presented by the Oakland Ballet from its 1965 inception through its spring 1990 season. The ballets are listed alphabetically by title, not counting a title's lead article such as *A, The, El, Le,* or *Les.* Thus, *Les Noces* is listed under *N,* and *Les Biches* under *B.* As the Oakland Ballet does not have a full set of house programs in its files, information for certain ballets is, as noted, incomplete.

ABRAHAM AND ISAAC
Choreographer: Dolores Delson
Music: Benjamin Britten (Canticle #2—Abraham and Isaac)
Premiere: September 28, 1973. Chabot College Auditorium, Hayward, Calif.
Cast: Rick Harper (Abraham), Dianne Brock (Isaac)

AFTERNOON OF A FAUN
Choreographer: Marc Wilde
Music: Claude Debussy
Premiere: June 3, 1972. Oakland Technical High School Auditorium. (First performed: 1968, Pacific Ballet.)
Cast: Ronn Guidi, Debbie Isaacson

AMIS
Choreographer: Ron Thiele
Music: Peter Ilyich Tchaikovsky (Trio in A minor, op. 50)
Costumes: Gillian Holaday
Premiere: October 22, 1982. Paramount Theatre, Oakland.
Cast: Michael Lowe, Abra Rudisill, Jon Konetski, Erin Leedom

ANOTHER DAY, ANOTHER DOLLAR
Choreographer: Zelda Mortimer
Music: Ahmad Jamal (The World is a Ghetto)
Costumes: Fran Stephens
Premiere: November 3, 1977. Zellerbach Auditorium, Berkeley.
Cast: Johanna Breyer (Flirty O'Feline), Danna Cordova (Insty O'Gater), Lance James (Sir Lancelot), Michael Lowe (Dynamite Lowe), Paul Mansa de Sousa (Hot Lips Sousa), Lynn Pendleton (St. Looney Lysol), Richard Smith (Trickster Dickster), Juli Stephens (Mother Earth), Ron Thiele (Big Rocky)

APOCALYPSE
Choreographer: Ronn Guidi
Music: Lubos Fisher and The Beatles
Premiere: October 1, 1971. Kaiser Center Auditorium, Oakland.
Cast: Dianne Brock, Ron Thiele, Tom Crocker

ARMENIAN DANCES
Choreographer: Ronn Guidi
Music: Aram Khachaturian

Premiere: March 18, 1972. Oakland Auditorium Theater.
Cast: Tricia Kaye, Raymond King

AT A TIME WHEN
Choreographer: Betsy Erickson
Music: Alan Hovhaness (Mountains and Rivers Without End)
Sculptural Pieces: Douglas Heine
Costumes: Sandra Woodall
Premiere: November 16., 1984. Zellerbach Auditorium, Berkeley.
Cast: Summer Lee Rhatigan, Allyson Deane, Joral Schmalle, Julie Lowe, Ron Thiele, Abra Rudisill, Mario Alonzo

AUBADE
Choreographer: Val Caniparoli
Music: Francis Poulenc
Costumes: Sandra Woodall
Premiere: September 12, 1986. Paramount Theater, Oakland. (First performed: 1986, Israel Ballet.)
Cast: Summer Lee Rhatigan, Allyson Deane, Ron Thiele, Erin Leedom, Mario Alonzo, Tally Frieder, David Kleine

THE AWAKENING
Choreographer: Emily Keeler
Sound Design: Richard Beggs (Ravel and Debussy piano pieces intervowen into score)
Costumes and Properties: Jacqueline Humbert
Premiere: September 30, 1988. Zellerbach Auditorium, Berkeley.
Cast: Abra Rudisill (The Woman), Ron Thiele (Her Husband), Patti Owen, Mario Alonzo (Two Lovers), Michael Lowe (The Woman's Lover), Jennifer Demko (A Child)

55

ABRA RUDISILL AND RICHARD CHEN IN RONN GUIDI'S *GALLOPS AND KISSES*

BALLADE

Choreographer: Ronn Guidi
Music: Chopin (Ballade in G minor)
Costumes: Fran Stephens
Premiere: October 11, 1980. Zellerbach Auditorium, Berkeley.
Cast: Shirlee Reevie, Ron Thiele

BEETHOVEN QUARTETS

Choreographer: John McFall
Music: Ludwig van Beethoven
Design: Victoria Gyorfi
Premiere: October 22, 1982. Paramount Theater, Oakland. (First performed: April 14, 1977, San Francisco Ballet.)
Cast: Erin Leedomm Jon Konetski, Julie Lowe, Michael Lowe, Shirlee Reevie, Ron Thiele

BELLA DI NOTTE

Choreographer: Tomm Ruud
Music: Sergei Prokofiev (Violin Concerto No. 2, Second Movement)
Costumes: John C. Gilkerson
Premiere: November 14, 1986. Zellerbach Auditorium, Berkeley.
Cast: Allyson Deane, Ron Thiele

LES BICHES

Choreographer: Bronislava Nijinska
Music: Francis Poulenc
Design: John C. Gilkerson after the original designs by Marie Laurencin
Premiere: September 24, 1982. Zellerbach Auditorium, Berkeley. (First performed: January 6, 1924, Diaghilev's Ballets Russes.)
Cast: Erin Leedom (Girl in Blue), Shirlee Reevie (Hostess), Lance James, Michael Lowe, Mario Alonzo (Athletes), Julie Lowe and Vicki Poston (Grey Girls)

BILLY THE KID

Choreographer: Eugene Loring
Music: Aaron Copland
Costumes: Richard Fletcher after Jared French
Sets: Susan Paigen after Jared French
Premiere: October 21, 1976. Zellerbach Auditorium, Berkeley. (First performed: October 16, 1938, Ballet Caravan.)
Cast: David McNaughton (Billy), Lance James (Pat Garrett), Michael Lowe (Alias), Patrice Whiteside (Mother/Sweetheart)
Note: Staged by Eugene Loring

BLUE DANUBE

Choreographer: Ronn Guidi
Music: Johann Strauss
Premiere: March 18, 1973. Oakland Auditorium Theater.
Cast: Dianne Brock, Judy Sandweiss, Tricia Kaye, Ronn Guidi, Robert Warner, John Tucker

BOLERO

Choreographer: Marc Wilde
Music: Maurice Ravel
Costumes: Stephen K. Simmons
Premiere: September 13, 1974. Paramount Theater, Oakland. (First performed: 1974, Pacific Ballet.)
Cast: Johanna Breyer, Dianne Brock, Tricia Kaye, Lynne Laakso, Carol Rheiner, Lynne Pendleton, Michael Lowe, Ron Thiele, Robert Warner

LA BOUTIQUE FANTASQUE

Choreographer: Léonide Massine
Music: Gioachinno Rossini, arranged by Ottorino Respighi
Design: André Derain
Premiere: October 26, 1978 (First performed: June 5, 1919, Diaghilev's Ballets Russes).
Cast: Arthur Conrad (Shopkeeper), Danna Cordova and Paul Manso de Sousa (Can-Can Dancers), Julie Zimmerman and Michael Lowe (the Poodles), Carol Rheiner and Lance James (Tarantella), David Blood (Snob), Ron Thiele (Cossack)
Note: Staged by Léonide Massine.

BRAHMS INTERMEZZI

Choreographer: Marc Wilde
Music: Johannes Brahms
Costumes: Michael David
Premiere: April 7, 1978. Paramount Theater, Oakland.
Cast: Michael Lowe and Carolyn Goto, Ron Thiele and Sally Streets, Lance James, and Danna Cordova

BRAHMS WALTZES

Choreographer: Charles Weidman (staged by Shela Xoregos).
Music: Johannes Brahms (Op. 39)
Costumes: Stephen K. Simmons (after Charles Weidman)
Premiere: September 12, 1986. Paramount Theater, Oakland. (First performed: June 12, 1967, Charles Weidman Co.)
Cast: Abra Rudisill, Patti Owen, Susan Taylor, Tally Frieder, Allyson Deane, Mario Alonzo, Michael Lowe, David Kleine

BRANDENBURG CONCERTO NO. 2 (also called CONCERTO IN F)

Choreographer: Ron Thiele

Music: J. S. Bach (Second and Third Movements)
Premiere: March 18, 1973. Oakland Auditorium Theater.
Cast: Michelle Attix, Charlotte Matinez, Terry Pedersen, Debbie Isaacson, Carol Rheiner, Lynne Laakso, Ron Thiele

BRANDENBURG CONCERTO NO. 3
Choreographer: Ron Thiele
Music: J. S. Bach
Costumes: Fran Stephens
Premiere: 1974. Oakland Auditorium Theater.
Cast: Lynn Pendeleton, Jackie Pavelich, Rick Harper, Lynne Laakso, Judy Sandweiss, Johanna Breyer.
Note: Exact date of premiere unknown.

THE BROOD
Choreographer: Richard Kuch
Music: Pierre Schaeffer
Costumes: Francois Barbeau, interpreted by Linda Trapp
Masks: Richard Ballet
Premiere: May 7, 1982. Zellerbach Auditorium, Berkeley. (First performed: 1968)
Cast: Jennifer Young (Mother Courage), Jon Konetski (Older son), Mario Alonzo (Younger Son), Deborah Pitts (Daughter).

CAKEWALK
Choreographer: Ruthanna Boris
Music: Louis Moreau Gottschalk, James Bland and anonymous minstrels: compiled by Paul Keuter and Ruthanna Boris
Costumes: Alan Madsen, after Robert Drew and Keith Martin
Set and Olio: Alan Madsen and Dale Haugo, after Jean Rosenthal and Robert Drew
Premiere: September 30,

1983. Zellerbach Auditorium, Berkeley. (First performed: June 12, 1951, New York City Ballet.)
Cast: Erin Leedom (Hortense), Carolyn Goto (The Wild Pony), Susan Taylor (Venus), Ron Thiele (Harolde), Michael Lowe (Louis the Illusionist), Abra Rudisill (Moreau), Joy Gim (Lesseau)

CAMILLE
Choreographer: Ronn Guidi
Music: Gabriel Pierne (Harp Rhapsody)
Costumes: Arthur Conrad
Premiere: Spring 1977.
Cast: Sally Streets (Marguarite), Lance James (Armand), Lynn Pendleton (Baron), John Sullivan (Armand's Father).
Note: Exact date and location of premiere unknown.

CARMEN SUITE
Choreographer: David McNaughton
Music: Georges Bizet
Premiere: June 13, 1976. Laney College Theater, Oakland.
Cast: Mindy Berrol, David McNaughton

CARMINA BURANA PAS DE DEUX
Choreographer: Ronn Guidi
Music: Carl Orff
Premiere: November 12, 1969. Veterans Auditorium (later Herbst Theater), San Francisco.
Cast: Dianne Brock, Ronn Guidi

CARMINA BURANA
Choreographer: Ronn Guidi
Music: Carl Orff
Premiere: May 11, 1973. Zellerbach Auditorium, Berkeley.
Cast: Tricia Kaye, Ronn Guidi,

Debbie Isaacson, Ron Thiele, Judy Sandweiss, Jack Yantis, Lynn Pendleton

CARMINA BURANA
Choreographer: John Butler
Music: Carl Orff
Costumes: John Butler
Premiere: September 20, 1985. Paramount Theater, Oakland. (First performed: 1959 New York City Opera.)
Cast: Erin Leedom, Jon Konetski, Summer Lee Rhatigan, Ron Thiele

CARNIVAL
Choreographer: Ronn Guidi
Music: Franz Liszt (Sixth Hungarian Rhapsody)
Premiere: October 15, 1970. Kaiser Center Auditorium, Oakland.
Cast: Dianne Brock, Lyla DeVita, Lisa Donaldson, Ronn Guidi, Lynn Pendleton, Ron Thiele

CARNIVAL D'AIX
Choreographer: Ronn Guidi
Music: Darius Milhaud
Costumes: John C. Gilkerson
Premiere: October 4, 1980. Zellerbach Auditorium, Berkeley.
Cast: Lance James, Michael Lowe, Mario Alonzo, Erin Leedom, Carol Rheiner, Gary Giffaune, Carolyn Goto, Silvio Briffa, Johanna Breyer, Shirlee Reevie, Ron Thiele

CHACONNE
Choreographer: Ron Thiele
Music: Antonio Vitali (transcribed by Ottorino Respighi)
Costumes: Fran Stephens
Premiere: May 4, 1974. Paramount Theater, Oakland.
Cast: Lynne Laakso, Ron Thiele

CHIMERA

Choreographer: Carlos
 Caravajal
Music: Luciano Berio
Premiere: May 23, 1970.
 Kaiser Center Auditorium,
 Oakland. (First performed:
 Dance Spectrum, 1969?)
Cast: Dianne Brock, Ronn
 Guidi

LE CID

Choreographer: Stephen K.
 Simmons
Music: Jules Massenet
Premiere: May 3, 1974. Oak-
 land Auditorium Theater.
Cast: Janet Carole, David
 Roland, Dianne Brock, John
 Sullivan, Judy Sandweiss,
 Ron Thiele

CONCERT WALTZES

Choreographer: Raoul Pausé
 and Marc Wilde
Music: Alexander Glazunov
Premiere: September 25,
 1965. Little Theater, Ber-
 keley. (First Performed:
 Oakland Civic Ballet, 1962)
Cast: Angene Feves, Ronn
 Guidi

CONCERTO GROSSO #1 IN G

Choreographer: Marc Wilde
Music: George Friderick
 Handel
Costumes: Jon Decon
Premiere: September 23, 1973.
 Chabot College Auditorium,
 Hayward, Calif.
Cast: Tricia Kaye, Lynne
 Laakso, Johanna Breyer,
 Janet Carole, Carol Rheienr,
 Lori Clausen, Ron Thiele,
 Rick Harper, Lynn Pendle-
 ton, David Roland, Jack
 Yantis, Jim Sohm

CONCERTO IN D

Choreographer: Raymond
 King
Music: J. S. Bach (Double

Violin Concerto)
Premiere: June 3, 1972. Oak-
 land Technical High School
 Auditorium.
Cast: Mary Keaveney, Dianne
 Brock, Ronn Guidi, Ray-
 mond King, Sheri Jack,
 Debbie Isaacson, Lynne
 Laakso, Ron Thiele

CONCIERTO DE ARANJUEZ

Choreographer: Ronn Guidi
Music: Joaquin Rodrigo
Premiere: See Note below.
Cast: See Note below.
Note: No program exists for
 this particular ballet. Ronn
 Guidi recalls staging it in
 1967 for the Oakland
 Ballet. It was first per-
 formed on May 17, 1965, for
 the Oakland Civic Ballet,
 with Ronn Guidi, Jaime
 Gomez, Anita Paciotti, and
 Angene Feves.

COPPELIA

Choreographer: Nicholas Ser-
 geyev, after Lev Ivanov and
 Enrico Cecchetti, which
 was in turn after Arthur
 Saint-Léon
Music: Léo Delibes
Sets: Richard Battle
Costumes: Fran Stephens
Premiere: September 24,
 1977. San Jose Center for
 the Performing Arts. (First
 peformed in this version:
 Vic-Wells Ballet, March 21,
 1933.)
Cast: Carol Rheiner (Swan-
 hilda), Lance James
 (Franz), Arthur Conrad (Dr.
 Coppelius)
Note: Staged by Jo Savino
 and Ann Jenner

CRYSTAL SLIPPER

Choreographer: Carlos
 Caravajal
Music: Bohuslav Martinu
 (Selections from Sextet for
 Winds and Piano, *Le Revue*

de Cuisine and *Spalicek*
 Suite, arranged by Carvajal)
Scenery and Costumes: Gerd
 Mairandres
Premiere: May 15, 1983. Para-
 mount Theater, Oakland.
 (First performed: 1977,
 Dance Spectrum.)
Cast: Erin Leedom (Cin-
 derella), Michael Lowe
 (Prince), Jennifer Young,
 Abra Rudisill (Stepsisters),
 Howard Sayette (Father),
 Douglas Hevenor (Step-
 mother), Mario Alonzo
 (Jester)

CRYSTALS

Choreographer: Ron Thiele
Music: Jeffrey Levine (Com-
 missioned Score)
Costumes: Ron Thiele
Premiere: September 19,
 1975. Paramount Theater,
 Oakland.
Cast: Johanna Breyer, Dianne
 Brock, Janet Carole,
 Michael Lowe, David
 McNaughton, Paul Sousa,
 Carol Rheiner, Stacey
 Swaner, Ron Thiele, Robert
 Warner

DAPHNIS AND CHLOE

Choreographer: Jean Paul
 Comelin
Music: Maurice Ravel
Costumes: Ann Marie Mar-
 szalkowski, John C.
 Gilkerson
Scenic Design: Roger LaVoie
Premiere: October 9, 1981.
 Paramount Theater, Oak-
 land. (First performed:
 1976, Milwaukee Ballet.)
Cast: Erin Leedom (Chloe),
 Michael Lowe (Daphnis),
 Lynne Domancie
 (Lycaenion), Lance James
 (Dorkon), Ron Thiele
 (Bryaxis)
Choreologist: Angela House

DEATH AND THE MAIDEN
Choreographer: Robert North (staged by Linda Gibbs)
Music: Franz Schubert
Costumes Interpreted by: John C. Gilkerson
Premiere: October 28, 1983. Paramount Theater, Oakland. (First performed: 1980, London Contemporary Dance Theatre.)
Cast: Erin Leedom, Ron Thiele

DEATH IN VENICE
Choreographer: John Pasqualetti
Music: Gerhard Samuel (Cold when the Drums Sound for Dawn)
Premiere: March 26, 1977. Laney College Theater, Oakland.
Cast: John Sullivan (Aschenbach), Raymond Johnson (The Stranger), Paul Sousa (Jaschu), Tricia Kaye (Tadzio's Mother), Lance James (Tadzio)

DENSITY 21
Choreographer: Jack Yantis
Music: Edgard Varèse (Density 21.5 for solo flute)
Premiere: March 3, 1974. Oakland Auditorium Theater.
Cast: Carol Rheiner (solo)

DIVERSIONS
Choreographer: Ron Thiele
Music: Benjamin Britten (Diversions for Piano Left Hand and Orchestra)
Costumes: Mario Alonzo
Premiere: October 23, 1987. Zellerbach Auditorium, Berkeley.
Cast: Julie Lowe, Tally Frieder, Patti Owen, Jennifer Demko, Joy Gim, Erin Leedom, Michael Lowe, Michael Myers, Mario Alonzo, Rafael Santiago, Pedro Barrios, Brad Bradley

DIVERTISSEMENT
Choreographer: Arthur Conrad
Music: Jacques Ibert (Divertissement)
Premiere: March 18, 1972. Oakland Auditorium Theater.
Cast: Dianne Brock, Susan Edgren, Tom Crocker, Tricia Kaye, Ron Thiele, Genene Rosen, Ronn Guidi, Gary Miner Lynn Pendleton, Sandra Young

DUO CONCERTANTE
Choreographer: John Pasqualetti
Music: Igor Stravinsky
Costumes: Mary Ann Seymour
Premiere: September 13, 1974. Paramount Theater, Oakland. (First performed 1973, Pacific Ballet.)
Cast: Sally Streets, John Loschmann (guest artist from Pacific Ballet)

DVORAK DANCES
Choreographer: Ronn Guidi
Music: Anton Dvorák (Prague Waltzes)
Costumes: Tricia Kaye
Premiere: September 24, 1982. Zellerbach Auditorium, Berkeley.
Cast: Ron Thiele, Shirlee Reevie, Lance James, Michael Lowe, Julie Lowe, Abra Rudisill, Erin Leedom

EPISODES
Choreographer: Ron Thiele
Music: Leos Janácek (Suite for String Orchestra, six movements)
Costumes: John C. Gilkerson
Premiere: October 28, 1983. Paramount Theatre, Oakland.
Cast: Erin Leedom, Summer Lee Rhatigan, Abra Rudisill, Jennifer Young, Mario Alonzo, Jon Konetski, Michael Lowe

FALL RIVER LEGEND
Choreographer: Agnes de Mille (staged by Enrique Martinez)
Music: Morton Gould
Costumes: Stanley Simmons
Sets: Oliver Smith
Premiere: September 26, 1986. Zellerbach Auditorium, Berkeley. (First performed: April 22, 1948, American Ballet Theatre.)
Cast: Summer Lee Ratigan (The Accused), Allyson Deane (Her Stepmother), Susan Taylor (Her Mother), Don Schwensen (Her Father), Ron Thiele (Her Pastor), Abra Rudisill (Herself as a Child), Erin Leedom and Mario Alonzo (Nocturne couple)

FANTASIA PARA UN GENTILHOMBRE
Choreographer: Ronn Guidi
Music: Joaquin Rodrigo
Entire Production Designed and Coordinated: John C. Gilkerson
Premiere: October 17. 1981. Paramount Theatre, Oakland.
Cast: Ron Thiele (The Gentleman), Sylvio Briffa (The Moor), Lynne Domancie (Moorish Girl), Johanna Breyer (Noblewoman), Lance James, Michael Lowe, Ian Leffler (Troubadours)

FANTASIES
Choreographer: John Clifford
Music: Ralph Vaughn Williams (Fantasia on a Theme by Thomas Tallis)
Costumes: Fran Stephens
Premiere: September 13, 1974. Paramount Theater, Oakland. (First performed: January 23, 1969, New York

Since joining the Oakland Ballet in 1969, Ron Thiele has served as one of the Company's leading dancers, resident choreographers, and currently its Associate Artistic Director. Thiele has contributed more than ten works to the Company's repertory, including "Amis" (opposite, top with Richard Chen-See, Joral Schmalle, and Jon Konetski), "How'd They Catch Me?" (opposite, bottom with Cynthia Chin and Joy Gim), and "Diversions" (below, with Joy Gim and Pedro Barrios).

City Ballet.)
Cast: Sally Streets and David
Roland (Older Couple), Lisa
Galloway and Jim Sohm
(Their Dreams)

FOREST
Choreographer: Ronn Guidi
Music: Franz Liszt
Premiere: May 23, 1970.
Kaiser Center Auditorium,
Oakland.
Cast: Sherri Jack, Reggy
Schmidt, Armando Angui-
ano, Ron Thiele

THE FOUNTAINS OF ROME
Choreographer: Ron Thiele
and Jack Yantis
Music: Ottorino Respighi
Premiere: March 3, 1974. Oak-
land Auditorium Theater.
Cast: Lynne Laakso, Stacey
Swaner, Jim Sohm, Johanna
Breyer, Jennifer Barnes,
Robert Warner, Jackie
Pavelich, Rick Harper, Lynn
Pendleton

FRAGMENT
Choreographer: Ronn Guidi
Music: Heitor Villa-Lobos
(Bachianas Brasileiras
No. 1)
Costumes: Stephen K. Sim-
mons
Sets: Rick Paul
Premiere: March 18, 1973.
Oakland Auditorium The-
ater.
Cast: Tricia Kaye (Sister), Ron
Thiele (Young Man), Judy
Sandweiss (Sister)

FUSION
Choreographer: Judith
Marcuss
Music: Pachelbel (Canon in D)
Design: Judith Marcuss
Premiere: May 10, 1974. Para-
mount Theater, Oakland.
Cast: Judy Sandwiess (The
Pulse), Tricia Kaye (A
Frightened Woman), Rick

Harper (A Bopper), Daivd
Roland, Jim Sohm (Mechan-
ical Men), Dianne Brock,
Robert Warner (Actors),
Lynne Laakso (A Searcher)

GALLOPS AND KISSES
Choreographer: Ronn Guidi
Music: Johann Strauss, Joseph
Lanner, Franz Schubert
Costumes: Richard Battle
Premiere: June 12, 1976.
Laney College Theater, Oak-
land.
Cast: Carolyn Goto, Carol
Rheiner, Julie Wilgus,
Danna Cordova, David
McNaughton, Lance James,
Michael Lowe, Lynn Pen-
dleton

GISELLE
Choreographer: Frederic
Franklin, after Jean Coralli,
Jules Perrot, and Marius
Petipa
Music: Adolphe Adam
Sets: Ron Steger
Costumes: Campbell Baird
and Christopher Thomsen
Premiere: October 9, 1987.
Paramount Theater, Oak-
land. (First performed:
June 28, 1841, Paris.)
Cast: Erin Leedom (Giselle),
Brad Bradley (Albrecht),
Ron Thiele (Hilarion); Patti
Owen and Mario Alonzo
(Peasant pas de deux), Joy
Gim (Myrtha), Cynthia Chin
and Patti Owen (Two Wilis)

GRAINGER SUITE
Choreographer: Ronn Guidi
Music: Percy Grainger:
Premiere: March 3, 1974. Oak-
land Auditorium Theater.
Cast: Julie Stephens, Max
Bolte, Lisa Galloway, Hugo
Blackwell, Mindy Berrol,
Douglas Heck, Jan Wexner,
Wayne Fleisher, Sima Wolf,
Michael Lowe, Dana Cor-
dova, Paul Sousa, Judy
Bean, Robert Hemmon,

Melenie Johnson, Tom
Pracher

GRAND TARANTELLA
Choreographer: Walter
Bourke
Music: Louis Gottschalk
Costumes: Walter Bourke
Premiere: September 19,
1975. Paramount Theater,
Oakland (First performed:
1974.)
Cast: Janet Carole, David
McNaughton

THE GREEN TABLE
Choreographer: Kurt Jooss
(staged by Anna Markard).
Libretto: Kurt Jooss
Music: Frederic (Fritz) A.
Cohen
Costumes: Hein Heckroth
Masks and Lightning: Her-
mann Markard
Premiere: September 21,
1984. Zellerbach Audito-
rium, Berkeley. (First per-
formed: July 3, 1932, Jooss
Ballet.)
Cast: Ron Thiele (Death), Jon
Konetski (Standard Bearer),
Richard Chen See (Profi-
teer), Don Schwennesen
(Old Soldier), Joral
Schmalle (Young Soldier),
Erin Leedom (Young Girl),
Allyson Deane (Mother),
Summer Lee Rhatigan
(Woman)

GYPSY
Choreographer: David
McNaughton
Music: David McNaughton
Costumes: Sandra Woodall
Premiere: October 6, 1989.
Paramount Theater, Oak-
land. (First performed: 1983
in original pas de deux ver-
sion; expanded version,
1985)
Cast: Joy Gim (The Gypsy),
Joral Schmalle (Her Lover),
Abra Rudisill, Michael
Lowe, Julie Cronshaw,

Jerome Vivona (Double pas de deux), Jill Taylor, Carlo Sierras, Pamela Lindsay (Pas de trois)

"HAND OF FATE" PAS DE DEUX FROM COTILLON

Choreographer: George Balanchine (recreated by Roman Jasinski and Moscelyne Larkin)
Music: Emmanuel Chabrier
Costumes: Dale Foster
Premiere: November 5, 1988. Campell Hall, University of California, Santa Barbara. (First performed: April 12, 1932, Ballet Russe de Monte Carlo.)
Cast: Joy Gim, Ron Thiele

HANSEL AND GRETEL

Choreographer: Ronn Guidi and Raoul Pausé
Music: Humperdinck, Hérold, Grieg
Design: Ernesti
Premiere: December 15, 1965. Kaiser Center Theater, Oakland. (First performed: Oakland Civic Ballet, 1963.)
Cast: Anita Paciotti (Gretel), Ronn Guidi (Hansel), Angene Feves (Dew Fairy), Don Erik (Cavalier)
Note: *Hansel and Gretel* was a constantly evolving ballet; by 1976 its musical collage included Hérold-Lanchberry (from *La Fille Mal Gardée*), Glazunov (*Scènes de Ballet, The Seasons*), Humperdinck (*Hansel and Gretel*) Lecocq *Mam-'zell Angot*), Handel (*Love in Bath*), Grieg (*Autumn Overture*)

HELP, HELP, THE GLOBOLINKS

Choreographer: Ronn Guidi
Music: Gian Carlo Menotti
Premiere: 1970 with Oakland Symphony

Note: No program exists, so exact date, location, and cast are not known.

HOLBERG SUITE

Choreographer: Raymond King
Music: Edvard Grieg
Premiere: March 18, 1972. Oakland Auditorium Theater.
Cast: Dianne Brock, Ronn Guidi, Tricia Kaye, Ron Thiele, Raymond King, Debbie Isaacson, Ann Aylor, Mary Keveaney, Lynne Laakso, Julie Ayala

HOW'D THEY CATCH ME?

Choreographer: Ron Thiele
Music: Igor Stravinsky (Two Suites for Small Orchestra)
Costumes: Lou-Anne Fauteck, Ron Thiele
Premiere: October 6, 1989. Paramount Theater, Oakland.
Cast: Cynthia Chin, Joy Gim, Jill Taylor, Susan Taylor, Abra Rudisill, Mario Alonzo, Michael Lowe, Joral Schmalle, Don Schwennsen

IN AUTUMN

Choreographer: Ronn Guidi
Music: Peter Ilyich Tchaikovsky (Roccoco Variations for Cello and Orchestra)
Design: John Gilkerson
Premiere: March 28, 1980. Paramount Theater, Oakland.
Cast: Erin Leedom and Lance James, Matthew Jessner and Mario Alonzo, Ron Thiele and Shirlee Reevie, Johanna Breyer and John Sullivan

INCONSEQUENTIALS

Choreographer: Agnes de Mille (staged by Ilene Strickler)
Music: Franz Schubert

(Allegro from Sonata in A Major #13, Das Wandren, Das Lieb im Grünen, Waltzes, The Blind Dance, and Du Bist die Ruhe)
Costumes: Santo Loquasto
Premiere: October 14, 1983. Zellerbach Auditorium, Berkeley. (First performed: Original version 1976, Boston Ballet; Final version 1981, Richmond Ballet.)
Cast: Erin Leedom, Jon Konetski, Abra Rudisill, Joral Schmalle, Michael Lowe, Diane Cassou

JARDIN AUX LILAS (LILAC GARDEN)

Choreographer: Antony Tudor (staged by Sallie Wilson)
Music: Ernest Chausson (*Poème*, op. 25)
Costumes: Hugh Stevenson
Set: Ron Steger
Premiere: September 16, 1988. Paramount Theater, Oakland. (First performed: January 26, 1936, Ballet Rambert.)
Cast: Abra Rudisill (Caroline), Michael Lowe (Her Lover), Ron Thiele (The Man She Must Marry), Susan Taylor (An Episode in His Past)

JAZZIANA

Choreographer: Marc Wilde
Music: Georg Phillipp Telemann
Premiere: April 7, 1966. Kaiser Center Auditorium, Oakland. (First performed: 1961, Pacific Ballet.)
Cast: Dianne Brock, Ronn Guidi, John DeLeon

JOHN FIELD

Choreographer: Ronn Guidi
Music: John Field (Piano Concerto No. 1)
Premiere: October 1, 1971. Kaiser Center Auditorium, Oakland.
Cast: Dianne Brock, Ronn

Since 1984, Betsy Erickson has served as the Oakland Ballet's ballet mistress and one of its resident choreographers. Erickson—who won wide praise as a dancer of impeccable precision and classic self-restraint during her years with American Ballet Theatre and the San Francisco Ballet—has shown herself to be a multifaceted choreographer. Her work for the Oakland Ballet has ranged from the exotically textured mixture of classical and modern dancing seen in "Waterways" (opposite, top with Joy Gim and Ron Thiele), to the light, bright, but technically challenging "Sfumato," Erickson's tribute to mentor Lew Christensen (below, with Susan Taylor, Hilary Wright, Ron Thiele, and Pedro Barrios). Among the other works Erickson has created for the Company is "Visions Fugitive" (opposite, bottom with Abra Rudisill and Michael Lowe).

Guidi, Genene Rosen, Gary Miner, Lynne Laakso, Ron Thiele

JUPITER
Choreographer: Ronn Guidi
Music: W. A. Mozart
Costumes: Fran Stephens
Premiere: August 1975. Concord Pavilion, Concord, Calif.
Cast: Dianne Brock, David McNaughton, Johanna Breyer, Sally Streets, Ron Thiele, Robert Warner, Tricia Kaye, Paul Stewart

LANDESCAPE
Choreographer: Ronn Guidi
Music: Robert Hughes (Commissioned Score, *Cones*)
Costumes: Fran Stephens
Set: Henrietta Berk
Premiere: September 19, 1975. Paramount Theater.
Cast: Tricia Kaye, Kathy Sim, Sally Streets, Ron Thiele, Lynn Pendleton, Robert Warner

LES LESQUERCARDES
Choreographer: Ronn Guidi
Music: Léo Delibes
Premiere: October 15, 1970. Kaiser Center Auditorium, Oakland.
Cast: Sheri Jack, Peggy Schmidt, Ron Thiele, John Sullivan

LOVE IN BATH
Choreographer: Charles Pierrier
Music: George Friderick Handel
Premiere: September 28, 1973. Oakland Auditorium Theater.
Cast: Cathy Sims, Charles Pierrier

LYNCHTOWN
Choreographer: Charles Weidman (staged by Shela Xoregos)

Music: Lehman Engel
Costumes: Stephen K. Simmons
Premiere: November 15, 1985. Zellerbach Auditorium, Berkeley. (First performed: 1936, Humphrey-Weidman Company.)
Cast: Abra Rudisill (Inciter), David Kleine (Victim), Jane Edwards, Tally Frieder, Erin Leedom, Dana sample, Susan Taylor, Mario Alonzo, Jon Konetski, Ian Leffler, Michael Lowe (Chorus)

MANDOLIN DREAM
Choreographer: David McNaughton
Music: J. S. Bach (Air from Suite No. 3), L. van Beethoven (Sonatina for harpsichord and mandolin), Camille Saint-Saens ("My Heart at thy sweet voice" from *Samson et Dalila*)
Costumes: Fran Stephens
Premiere: October 2, 1976. Laney College, Oakland.
Cast: Michael Lowe, Tricia Kaye, Carol Rheiner, Janet Carole

MORNING SONG
Choreographer: Ronn Guidi
Music: Edward Elgar
Premiere: May 23, 1970. Kaiser Center Auditorium, Oakland.
Cast: Dianne Brock, Ronn Guidi

MOZART FOR EIGHT
Choreographer: Peter Nel
Music: W. A. Mozart (Ballet Music from *Idomeneo*)
Premiere: June 12, 1976. Laney College Theater, Oakland.
Cast: Sally Streets, Tricia Kaye, Laura Brown, Janet Carole, Peter Nel, Ron Thiele, Robert Warner, David McNaughton

NICHOLAS AND CONCEPCION (Excerpts from Act II)
Choreographer: Ronn Guidi
Music: Gerhard Samuel (commissioned score)
Costumes: Mario Alonzo
Premiere: November 13, 1987. Zellerbach Auditorium, Berkeley.
Cast: Ron Thiele (Nicholas) Erin Leedom (Concepcion)

LES NOCES
Choreographer: Bronislava Nijinska
Music: Igor Stravinsky
Design: Natalie Gontcharova
Premiere: September 25, 1981. Zellerbach Auditorium, Berkeley. (First performed: June 13, 1923, Diaghilev's Ballets Russes.)
Cast: Johanna Breyer (Bride), Mylene Kalhorn, Philip Sharper (Groom), Lance James, Erin Leedom, Joy Gim, Mario Alonzo, Michael Lowe
Note: Choreologist, Juliette Kando, The Royal Ballet; production overseen by Irina Nijinska

THE NUTCRACKER
Choreographer: Ronn Guidi
Music: Peter Ilyich Tchaikovsky
Sets: Rick Paul
Costumes: Stephen K. Simmons
Premiere: December 1972. Medford High School Auditorium, Medford, Oregon. First Oakland performance: December 19, 1973, Paramount Theater. (First performed in Ivanov's version: December 17, 1892, Maryinsky Theatre.)
Cast of first Oakland Performance: Jim Sohm (Nephew), Arthur Conrad (Drosselmeyer), Lynne Laakso (Dream Marie),

Janet Carole and Michael Cappara (Snow Queen and Snow King), Tricia Kaye and Ron Thiele (Sugarplum Fairy and Cavalier), Dianne Brock and David Roland (Rose and Cavalier), Ramon Galindo (Licorice), Judy Marcuss (Dancing Doll)

OPUS 29: IN MEMORIAM BENJAMIN BRITTEN
Choreographer: David L. Lopes
Music: Benjamin Britten (Prelude and Fugue, Opus 29)
Costumes: Fran Stephens
Premiere: March 26, 1977. Laney College Theater, Oakland.
Cast: Lisa Rae, Michael Lowe, Sheri Skiles, Lynn Pendleton, Stacy Swaner, Paul Sousa

PARTITA FOR FOUR
Choreographer: Gerald Arpino (staged by James Howell)
Music: Vittorio Rieti
Costumes: Peter Anthony (aka Gerald Arpino)
Premiere: September. 6, 1974. Paramount Theater, Oakland. (First performed: May 18, 1961, Joffrey Ballet.)
Cast: Lisa Galloway, Jim Sohm, Ron Thiele, David Roland

PAS DE QUATRE
Choreographer: Anton Dolin (after Jules Perrot)
Music: Cesare Pugni
Premiere: October 1, 1976. Laney College Theater, Oakland. (First performed: July 12, 1845, Her Mejesty's Theatre, London. Dolin's reconstruction first performed: 1941, American Ballet Theatre.)
Cast: Carolyn Goto, Tricia Kaye, Sally Streets, Christine Walton
Note: Staged by Sally Streets

PAS DE TROIS IN A NEO-CLASSIC MODE
Choreographer: Larry Burgoon
Music: J. C. Bach (Sinfonia, op. 6, no. 6)
Premiere: June 11, 1976. Laney College Theater, Oakland.
Cast: Sally Streets, Janet Carole, Robert Warner

PAS DE TROIS
Choreographer: Sally Streets
Music: Carl Maria von Weber (Andante and Hungarian Rondo)
Costumes: Sally Streets and Sandra Woodall
Premiere: April 5, 1980. Paramount Theater, Oakland.
Cast: Lance James, Carolyn Goto, Daniel Ray

PEAR
Choreographer: Jack Yantis
Music: Erik Satie (Three Pieces in the Shape of a Pear)
Premiere: September 28, 1973. Oakland Auditorium Theater.
Cast: Janet Carole, Dianne Brock, Judy Sandwiess, Tricia Kaye, Ron Thiele, Ronn Guidi, John Tucker, Lynn Pendleton

PETER AND THE WOLF
Choreographer: Ronn Guidi
Music: Sergei Prokofiev
Premiere: April 5, 1966. Kaiser Center Auditorium, Oakland. (First performed October 27, 1963, Oakland Civic Ballet.)
Cast: Ronn Guidi, Dianne Brock, Wendy Reynolds, Anita Paciotti, Arthur Conrad

PETER AND THE WOLF
Choreographer: Ronn Guidi
Music: Sergei Prokofiev
Costumes and Sets: Margo Humphrey
Premiere: May 11, 1990. Paramount Theater, Oakland.
Cast: Mario Alonzo (Peter), Abra Rudisill (Bird), Joy Gim (Duck), Michael Lowe (Cat), Don Schwennesen (Grandfather), Ron Thiele (Wolf), Ben Burnhurt, Scott Warren, Omar Shabazz (Hunters), Danny Glover (Narrator)

LES PETITS RIENS
Choreographer: Ron Thiele and Ronn Guidi
Music: W. A. Mozart
Premiere: 1978. Alameda High, Alameda, Calif.
Cast: Carolyn Goto, Lance James, Michael Lowe, Joni Jaclobs, Shirlee Reevie, Paul Sousa
Note: Exact date unknown.

PETRUSHKA
Choreographer: Stephen Simmons
Music: Igor Stravinsky
Design: Rick Paul
Premiere: May 4, 1974. Paramount Theater, Oakland.
Cast: Ron Thiele (Petrushka, a rock star), John Sullivan (Serge, his producer), Jack Yantis (Rome, a pusher), Janet Carole (Chimera, a groupie), Dianne Brock (Luxa, a rich admirer)

POLOVETSIAN DANCES FROM PRINCE IGOR
Choreographer: Michel Fokine (staged by Frederic Franklin)
Music: Alexander Borodin
Scenery and Costumes: Nicholas Roerich, courtesy of Indianapolis Ballet Theatre
Premiere: October 8, 1982. Paramount Theater, Oakland. (First performed: May 19, 1909, Diaghilev's Ballets Russes.)

Cast: Julie Lowe (Small girl), Ron Thiele (Polovetsian Warrior), Shirlee Reevie (Polovetsian Woman), Mario Alonzo, Michael Lowe, Richard Chen See, Greg Gonzales (Warriors)

POLOVETZIAN DANCES

Choreographer: Ronn Guidi
Music: Alexander Borodin (Dances from *Prince Igor*)
Costumes: Daniel Lordon
Premiere: March 18, 1973. Oakland Auditorium Theater.
Cast: Judy Sandweiss, Tricia Kaye, Dianne Brock, Debbie Issacson, Carol Rheiner, Tom Crocker, Terry Koch, Lynn Pendleton, Charlotte Martinez, Michelle Attix, Daniel Lordon, Ronn Guidi, Johanna Breyer, Sonj Ramsey, Juli Stephens, Jack Yantis

THE PROPOSAL OF PANTALONE

Choreographer: Angene Feves
Music: Marin Marais and D'Herveloix (Suites for Harpischord and Viola da Gamba)
Sets: Joan Larkey
Costumes: E. Andreina
Premiere: September 25, 1965. Little Theater, Berkeley. (First performed: Oakland Civic Ballet, May 29, 1965.)
Cast: Angene Feves, Anita Paciotti, Jaime Gomez, Arthur Conrad, Marcia Olson, Ronn Guidi

PURSUIT OF HAPPINESS

Choreographer: May O'Donnell
Music: Big Band Hits from the 1930s and '40s
Costumes: Frank Shawl
Premiere: September 15, 1989. Paramount Theater, Oakland. (First performed: 1977, May O'Donnell Dance Company.)
Cast: Susan Taylor, Abra Rudisill, Jill Taylor, Joy Gim, Cynthia Chin, Scott Warren, Mario Alonzo
Note: Staged by Frank Shawl. Reconstructed by Barbara Allegra Verlezza and Sabatino Verlezza

QUIET CITY

Choreographer: Ronn Guidi
Music: Aaron Copland
Costumes: Fran Stephens
Premiere: March 21, 1971. Oakland Auditorium Theater.
Cast: Margaret Schmidt, Ron Thiele, Barbara Staggers, Lynn Pendleton

QUIET CITY

Choreographer: David Blood
Music: Aaron Copland
Premiere: March 18, 1976. Choreographer's Workshop, Oakland Auditorium Theater.
Cast: Lance James, Kabby Mitchell III, Paul Stewart, Stacy Swaner, Patrice Whiteside

RAGS

Choreographer: Ronn Guidi
Music: Scott Joplin
Costumes: Fran Stephens
Premiere: April 28, 1973. Chabot College Theater, Hayward, Calif.
Cast: Lynn Pendleton, Stacey Swaner (Pine Apple Rag), Ronn Guidi, Lynn Pendleton, Jack Yantis (The Entertainer), with Jennifer Barnes, Judy Bean, Mindy Berrol, Joanna Breyer, Dana Cordova, Lisa Galloway, Melerie Johnson, Julie Stephens, Jan Wexner, Hugo Blackwell, Rick Harper, David Roland, John Tucker, Robert Warner

RAVEL PIANO CONCERTO (also called RAVEL PAS DE DEUX)

Choreographer: Ron Thiele
Music: Maurice Ravel (Second Movement)
Costumes: Lynne Laasko
Premiere: September 27, 1975. Paramount Theater, Oakland.
Cast: Laura Brown, Ron Thiele

RAYMONDA: CORTEGE HONGROIS

Choreographer: Stephen K. Simmons
Music: Alexander Glazunov
Costumes: Stephen K. Simmons
Sets: Andrew Ward
Premiere: September 23, 1973. Chabot College Auditorium, Hayward, Calif.
Cast: Janet Carole, Ron Thiele

REQUIEM

Choreographer: Ronn Guidi
Music: Gabriel Fauré
Costumes: Virginia Vandergift
Premiere: March 21, 1971. Oakland Auditorium Theater.
Cast: Ron Thiele (Christ), Ronn Guidi (Adam), Dianne Brock (Eve)
Note: A Fauré Requiem pas de deux premiered on October 2, 1966, with Anita Paciotti and Ronn Guidi

RESPIGHI DANCES

Choreographer: Ronn Guidi
Music: Ottorino Respighi
Costumes: Ernesti
Sets: Duke McLane
Premiere: April 5, 1966. Kaiser Center Auditorium, Oakland. (First performed October 27, 1963, Oakland Civic Ballet.)
Cast: Dianne Brock, Ronn Guidi, Jaime Gomez, Arthur Conrad

RESURRECTION

Choreographer: John
  Pasqualetti
Music: Igor Stravinsky
  ("Introitus," "Requiem
  Canticles")
Premiere: April 1, 1977.
  Laney College Theater, Oak-
  land.
Cast: Lance James, Paul
  Sousa, John Sullivan,
  Robert Warner; Michael
  Lowe; Danna Cordova,
  Tricia Kaye, Sally Streets,
  Stacy Swaner

THE RITE OF SPRING

Choreographer: John
  Pasqualetti
Music: Igor Stravinsky
Costumes: Rob Blackman—
  later listed as John
  Pasqualetti
Sets: Rob Blackman
Premiere: April 7, 1978. Para-
  mount Theater, Oakland.
Cast: Tom Cockerline, Danna
  Cordova, Carolyn Goto, Joni
  Jacobson, Lance James,
  Matthew Jessner, Michael
  Lowe, Paul Manso de Sousa,
  Shirley Reevie, Carol
  Rheiner, Sheri Skiles,
  Richard Smith, Ron Thiele,
  Martin Weber, Jennifer
  Young

RODEO: FOUR DANCE EPISODES

Choreographer: Paul Stewart
Music: Aaron Copland
Premiere: March 8, 1976.
  Choreographer's Workshop,
  Oakland Auditorium
  Theater.
Cast: David Blood, Paul
  Stewart, Judith Bean,
  Margo Scharlin, Michael
  Lowe, Robert Warner, Carol
  Rheiner, Stacy Swaner, Paul
  Sousa, Patricia Whiteside

ROMANIAN DANCES

Choreographer: Jim Piersall
Music: Bela Bartok

Costumes: Fran Stephens
Premiere: March 18. 1973.
  Oakland Auditorium The-
  ater.
Cast: Dianne Brock, Debbie
  Isaacson, Lynne Laakso,
  Tom Crocker, Ramon
  Galindo, Lynn Pendleton

ROOMS

Choreographer: Anna
  Sokolow
Music: Kenyon Hopkins
Costumes: Fran Stephens
Premiere: March 28, 1980.
  Paramount Theater, Oak-
  land. (First performed:
  February 24, 1955, Sokolow
  Company.)
Cast: Ron Thiele, Shirlee
  Reevie, Michael Lowe,
  Lance James, Patrice
  Whiteside, Erin Leedom,
  Julie Zimmerman, Jennifer
  Young, David Blood

EL SALON MEXICO

Choreographer: Robert
  Warner
Music: Aaron Copland
Premiere: March 8, 1976
  Choreographer's Workshop,
  Oakland Auditorium
  Theater.
Cast: Michael Lowe, Paul
  Stewart, Laura Brown,
  Carol Rheiner, Paul Mansa
  de Sousa, Robert Warner,
  Tricia Kaye, Stacey Swaner

EL SALON MEXICO

Choreographer: Ronn Guidi
Music: Aaron Copland
Costumes: Fran Stephens
Backdrop by Henrietta Burk
Premiere: May 14, 1980.
  Detroit, Michigan.
Cast: Carolyn Goto, Jeff
  Hughes, Johanna Breyer,
  Ron Thiele, Michael Lowe,
  Sylvio Briffa, Madonna
  Clift, Ian Leffler, Deborah
  Pitts, Charol Rheiner

SANCTUM

Choreographer: Irine Nadel

Music: Environmental Sounds
Costumes: Lisa Theilhammer
Premiere: October 1, 1976.
  Laney College Theater, Oak-
  land.
Cast: Janet Carole, David
  McNaughton, Danna Cor-
  dova, Carol Rheiner, Lance
  James, Sheri Skiles, Tricia
  Kaye, Julie Zimmerman,
  Michale Lowe, Lance James

SEASCAPE

Choreographer: Ronn Guidi
Music: Aaron Copland (Clari-
  net Concerto, Second Move-
  ment)
Premiere: June 11, 1976.
  Laney College Theater, Oak-
  land. (First performed:
  1975, Central Valley Ballet,
  Turlock, Calif.)
Cast: Erin Leedom, Lance
  James with Erin Bristow,
  Susan Taylor

THE SEASONS (SELECTIONS)

Choreographer: Ronn Guidi
  and Raoul Pausé
Music: Alexander Glazunov
Costumes: Sandra Woodall
Premiere: November 15, 1985.
  Zellerbach Auditorium, Ber-
  keley. (First performed:
  1963, Oakland Civic Ballet.)
Cast: Julie Lowe, Michael
  Lowe, Abra Rudisill, Mario
  Alonzo, Erin Leedom, Ron
  Thiele, Allyson Deane, Don
  Schwennesen, Patti Owen,
  Jon Konetski, Summer Lee
  Rhatigan

SEMIRAMIDE

Choreographer: Ronn Guidi
Music: Gioacchino Rossini
Premiere: March 18, 1972.
  Oakland Auditorium The-
  ater.
Cast: Tricia Kaye, Dianne
  Brock, Debbie Isaacson,
  Ron Thiele, Ronn Guidi,
  Raymond King, Lynne
  Laakso, Tom Crocker, Julia
  Ayala

SFUMATO
Choreographer: Betsy Erickson
Music: Luigi Boccherini (Cello Concerto No. 2)
Costumes: Sandra Woodall
Premiere: November 14, 1986. Zellerbach Auditorium, Berkeley.
Cast: Erin Leedom, Abra Rudisill, Susan Taylor, Allyson Deane, Julie Lowe, Summer Lee Rhatigan, Mario Alonzo, Michael Lowe, Hilary Wright, Pedro Barrios, Ron Thiele

SHAPES OF EVENING
Choreographer: Carlos Carvajal
Music: Claude Debussy (Danse Sacrée et Profane)
Costumes: Fran Stephens
Premiere: March 27, 1977. Laney College Theater, Oakland. (First performed: August 4, 1967, San Francisco Ballet.)
Cast: Janet Carole, Tom Cockerline, Sally Streets, Michael Lowe, Stacey Swaner, Lance James

SHEHERAZADE
Choreographer: Michel Fokine (staged by Nicolas Beriozoff)
Music: Nicolai Rimsky-Korsakov
Design: Léon Bakst (realized by John C. Gilkerson)
Premiere: November 9, 1979. Paramount Theater, Oakland. (First performed: June 4, 1910, Diaghilev's Ballets Russes.)
Cast: Sally Streets (Zobeide), Ron Thiele (The Golden Slave), Howard Sayette (The Shah), Lance James (The Shah's Brother), David Blood (The Eunuch)

SIBELIUS
Choreographer: Ronn Guidi

Music: Jean Sibelius (Fifth Symphony)
Costumes: Fran Stephens
Premiere: August 12, 1978. Palace of Fine Arts, San Francisco.
Cast: Patrice Whiteside, Joni Jacobson, Shirley Reevie, Johanna Breyer, Ron Thiele, Lance James, Michael Lowe, Matthew Jessner, Carol Rheiner, Carolyn Goto, Erin Leedom, Danna Cordova, Chris Hoskins, Tom Cockerline, David Blood, Paul Manso de Sousa

SILENT SPRING (also called ENCOUNTER)
Choreographer: Raymond King
Music: Patrick Williams
Premiere: June 3, 1972. Oakland Technical High School Auditorium.
Cast: Dianne Brock, Raymond King

THE SIRENS
Choreographer: Marc Wilde
Music: Claude Debussy
Set: Jacques Bloxham
Costumes: Michael David
Premiere: April 7, 1978. Paramount Theater, Oakland.
Cast: Danna Cordova, Lance James, Paul Sousa, Michael Lowe

THE SISTERS
Choreographer: Eugene Loring
Music: Carl Ruggles
Design: Don Bradburn
Premiere: November 3, 1977. Zellerbach Auditorium, Berekely. (First performed: 1966, San Diego Ballet.)
Cast: Tricia Kaye (Eldest Sister), Patrice Whiteside (Second Sister), Janet Carole (Third Sister), Julie Zimmerman (Youngest Sister), Lance James

(Brother), Lynn Pendleton (Minister), Michael Lowe (Gentleman Caller)

SLOE GIN
Choreographer: Rachael Harms
Music: Yancy, Lewis and The Dixie Four
Premiere: March 28, 1980. Paramount Theater, Oakland. (First performed: 1977, Dance Kaleidoscope.)
Cast: Carolyn Goto, Carol Rheiner, Sherry Rodwell, Johanna Breyer, Shirlee Reevie

THE SNOW MAIDEN (also known as LE SOLEIL DE NUIT)
Choreographer: Léonide Massine
Music: Rimsky-Korsakov
Premiere: November 9, 1979. Paramount Theater, Oakland. (First performed: December 20, 1915, Diaghilev's Ballets Russes.)
Cast: Shirlee Reevie (Snow Maiden), Lance James (Midnight Sun), Carolyn Goto (Beaver), Mathew Jessner and David Blood (Hunters)
Note: Staged by Léonide Massine

LE SOIR
Choreographer: Sally Streets
Music: Franz Joseph Hayden (Symphony No. 8)
Costumes: Sally Streets
Premiere: April 4, 1981. Paramount Theater, Oakland. (First performed: 1980.)
Cast: Julie Zimmerman, Michael Lowe, Erin Leedom, Lance James, Mylene Kalhorn, Robert Nichols

SOIREE MUSICALE
Choreographer: Ronn Guidi
Music: Giaocchino Rossini/ Benjamin Britten

Costumes: Fran Stephens
Premiere: March 21, 1971.
Oakland Auditorium Theater.
Cast: Dianne Brock, Ron Thiele, Susan Edgren, Wendy Burns, Lyla DeVita, Terry Koch, John Sullivan, Margaret Schmidt, Sheri Jack

A SOLDIER'S TALE

Choreographer: Arthur Conrad and Ronn Guidi
Music: Igor Stravinsky
Costumes: Rick Paul
Premiere: March 9, 1975. Zellerbach Hall, Berkeley.
Cast: Arthur Conrad (Narrator), Ron Thiele (Soldier), Rick Harper (Devil), Dianne Brock (Princess)

SONATA

Choreographer: Betsy Erickson
Music: Tommaso Albioni (Sonata for harpsichord and strings, op. 2, no. 6)
Costumes: Sandra Woodall
Premiere: October 14, 1983. Zellerbach Auditorium, Berkeley.
Cast: Summer Lee Rhatigan, Carolyn Goto, Erin Leedom, Ron Thiele, Michael Lowe, Jon Konetski

LE SPECTRE DE LA ROSE

Choreographer: Michel Fokine (staged by Anatole Vilzak)
Music: Carl Maria von Weber (Invitation to the Dance)
Costumes: Fran Stephens
Sets: John Gilkerson
Premiere: October 2, 1976 (First Performed April 19, 1911, Diaghilev's Ballets Russes.)
Cast: Janet Carole, David McNaughton

STAR JOURNEY

Choreographer: Jack Yantis

Music: Frank Ahrold (commissioned score)
Design: Rick Paul
Premiere: September 26, 1975. Paramount Theater, Oakland.
Cast: Kirsten Anderson, Judy Bean, Rachel Brumer, David Blood, Max Bolte, Michael Lowe, Deborah Palesch, Paul Sousa, Juli Stephens, Robert Warner, Tom Pracher, Jan Wexner, Patrice Whiteside

STREET SONGS

Choreographer: Val Caniparoli
Music: Carl Orff
Premier: October 16, 1983. Zellerbach Auditorium, Berkeley. (First performed: 1980 Pacific Northwest Ballet.)
Cast: Michael Lowe, Erin Leedom, Mario Alonzo, Susan Taylor, Douglas Hevenor, Summer Lee Rhatigan, Abra Rudisill, Michael Myers, Jon Konetski, Jennifer Young

A STREETCAR NAMED DESIRE

Choreographer: John Pasqualetti
Music: Alex North (from his score for Elia Kazan's movie)
Costumes: Mary Ann Seymour
Premiere: May 3, 1974. Paramount Theater, Oakland.
Cast: Tricia Kaye (Blanche), Judy Sandweiss (Stella), Ron Thiele (Stanley Kowalski), John Sullivan (Mitch and Cameraman), Jim Sohm (Blanche's Husband)

SYLVIA SUITE

Choreographer: Raoul Pausé
Music: Léo Delibes
Premiere: September 25, 1965. Little Theater, Berkeley. (First Performed: Oakland Civic Ballet, May

29, 1965.)
Cast: Dianne Brock, Ronn Guidi, Antia Paciotti, Susan Edgren
Note: The September 25, 1965, program cannot be found, so this is the May 29, 1965 cast)

SYNERGIES

Choreographer: Carlos Carvajal
Music: Sergei Prokofiev (Piano Concerto No. 5)
Costumes: Carvajal, Houser, Seymour
Premiere: October 26, 1984. Paramount Theater, Oakland.
Cast: Summer Lee Rhatigan, Don Schwennesen, Susan Taylor, Sean Ramirez, Joy Gim, Daniel Ray, Abra Rudisill, Richard Chen See, Julie Lowe, Patti Owen, Mario Alonzo, Erin Leedom, Joral Schmalle, Allyson Deane, Robert Aames

TAR MARMALADE

Choreographer: Val Caniparoli
Music: Doug Adams (Tar Marmalade)
Costumes: Sandra Woodall
Premiere: October 12, 1984. Paramount Theatre, Oakland.
Cast: Summer Lee Rhatigan, Don Schwennesen

THE TENDER LAND

Choreographer: Eugene Loring
Music: Aaron Copland (Suite from the Opera The Tender Land)
Design: Robert Fletcher
Premiere: October 20, 1978. Paramount Theater, Oakland.
Cast: Patrice Whiteside (Laurie), Ron Thiele (Grandfather), Lance James (Martin the Drifter), Jennifer Young (Mother), Julie

Throughout its history, the Oakland Ballet has been a showcase for contemporary California choreographers, such as Emily Keeler, who in 1988 created "The Awakening" (opposite, top with Abra Rudisill). Other California choreographers who have worked with the Company include Carlos Carvajal, whose most recent ballet for the Company is "Synergies" (opposite, bottom with Robert Aames and Alyson Deane), and Tandy Beal, a modern choreographer who, in 1984, created ". . . this harsh spectacle, this invisible activity, this sense . . ." (below, with Abra Rudisill).

Zimmerman (Beth)
Note: Aaron Copland conducted premiere.

. . . THIS HARSH SPECTACLE, THIS INVISIBLE ACTIVITY, THIS SENSE . . .

Choreographer: Tandy Beal
Music: John Scoville
Costumes: Elaine Yokoyama-Roos
Sets: Norvid Roos
Premiere: October 12, 1984. Paramount Theater, Oakland.
Cast: Robert Aames, Mario Alonzo, Richard Chen See, Allyson Deane, Jane Edwards, Erin Leedom, Julie Lowe, Patti Owen, Abra Rudisill, Joral Schmalle, Susan Taylor, Ron Thiele, and children of Oakland Ballet Academy

THIS POINT IN TIME

Choreographer: Brenda Way
Music: Conrad Cummings (Fantasy on Beach Boys' "I Wish They All Could Be . . .")
Design: Wayne Thiebaud
Premiere: September 18, 1987. Paramount Theater, Oakland.
Cast: Creators: Tally Frieder, Joy Gim, Lelsie Ann Larson, Mario Alonzo, Vincent Cowart, Ron Thiele; Subjects: Patti Owen (Wife), Frank Everett (Husband), Julie Lowe (Child), Pedro Barrios (Artist)

TIME UNTO TIME

Choreographer: Eugene Loring
Music: Bela Bartok (Music for Strings, Percussion, and Celeste)
Costumes: Fran Stephens
Premiere: April 5, 1980. Paramount Theater, Oakland.
Cast: Chris Hoskin and

Madonna Clift, Lance James and Sherry Rodwell, Matthew Jessner and Jennifer Briffa, Ron Thiele and Patrice Whiteside

TIMES PAST

Choreographer: Keith Lee
Music: Cole Porter, Scott Joplin
Costumes: Marcos Paredes
Set: Oliver Smith
Premiere: September 26, 1975. Paramount Theater. (First performed July 1, 1970, American Ballet Theatre.)
Cast: David McNaughton (Shoe Shine Boy), Tricia Kaye (The Vamp), Robert Warner, Paul Sousa (Street Boys), Juli Stephens, Lynn Pendleton (At the Hop), Michael Lowe (Alone at the Dance), Stacey Swaner, Laura Brown (Passing Parade)

TOUCH

Choreographer: Ronn Guidi
Music: Ocean Waves and Gregorian Chants (Tape Montage by Wahlberg Studio)
Premiere: October 1, 1971. Kaiser Center Auditorium, Oakland.
Cast: Jeanne Hanna, Doreen Irby, Julie Ayala, Debbie Isaacson, Mary Keaveney, Lynne Laakso, Pat Muellner, Barbara Staggers, Gary Miner, Michael Kingsley, Dorn Yoder, Marc Martin, Lynn Pendleton

LE TRAIN BLEU

Choreographer: Bronislava Nijinska
Music: Darius Milhaud
Original Decor: Henri Laurens, realized by Ron Steger
Original Curtain: Pablo Picasso, realized by Ron Steger

Original Costumes: Gabrielle "Coco" Chanel, realized by Mario Alonzo and Dale Foster
Premiere: November 10, 1989. Berkeley Community Theater. (First performed: June 20, 1924, Diaghilev's Ballets Russes.)
Cast: Susan Taylor (A Tennis Champion), Abra Rudisill (Perlouse), Beau Gosse (Michael Lowe), Don Schwennesen (The Golfer)
Note: Preliminary reconstruction by Sir Anton Dolin and Frank W. D. Ries. Reconstructed, staged, and directed for Oakland Ballet by Irina Nijinska and Frank W. D. Ries after choreography by Bronislava Nijinska.

TRIBUTE

Choreographer: Frederic Franklin
Music: César Franck (Symphonic Variations)
Costumes: Mario Alonzo
Premiere: November 11. 1988. Paramount Theater, Oakland. (First performed: 1959, Ballet Russe de Monte Carlo.)
Cast: Patti Owen, Brad Bradley, Susan Taylor, Ron Thiele, Joy Gim, Don Schwennesen

TRIGGER

Choreographer: John McFall
Music: Philip Glass (Music in Twelve Parts, Part 1)
Costumes: Warren Travis
Premiere: October 4, 1985. Zellerbach Auditorium, Berkeley.
Cast: Julie Lowe, Abra Rudisill, Susan Taylor, Mario Alonzo, Jon Konetski, Joral Schmalle, Don Schwennesen

TROIS GYMNOPEDIES

Choreographer: Ronn Guidi

Music: Erik Satie
Premiere: April 7, 1966.
Kaiser Center Auditorium,
Oakland. (First performed:
1961, Oakland Civic Ballet.)
Cast: Dianne Brock, Helene
Krushwitz, Ronn Guidi

TWO OUT OF "FOUR"
Choreographer: Jack Yantis
Music: Maurice Ravel (String
Quartet, Second and Third
Movements)
Premiere: September 26,
1975. Paramount Theater,
Oakland.
Cast: Johanna Breyer, David
McNaughton, Janet Carole,
Lynn Pendleton, Susan
Magno, Ron Thiele, Deborah
Palesch, Robert Warner

UIRAPURU
Choreographer: Ronn Guidi
Music: Heitor Villa-Lobos
Costumes and Scenic Designs:
James Parra
Premiere: September 25, 1965.
Berkeley Little Theater.
Cast: Angene Feves (Uirapuru
the Bird), Jaime Gomez
(Uirapuru the Man), Dianne
Brock (The Maiden)

THE UNICORN, THE
GORGON, AND THE
MANTICORE
Choreographer: Ronn Guidi
Music: Gian Carlo Menotti
Design: Rick Paul
Premiere: March 9, 1975. Zeller-
bach Auditorium, Oakland.
Cast: Rick Harper (Man in the
Castle), Paul Manso de
Sousa (Unicorn), Ron Thiele
(Gorgon), Michael Lowe
(Manticore), Tricia Kaye
(Countess), John Sullivan
(Count), Judith Sandweiss
(Mayor's Wife), Paul Stew-
art (Mayor), Mindy Berrol
(Doctor's Wife), Robert
Warner (Doctor); January
22, 1967: Dianne Brock
(Unicorn), Don Springer
(Gorgon), Arthur Conrad

(Manticore), William Couser
(the Man in the Castle),
Arthur Conrad, Angene
Feves (Count and Count-
ess), Sven Karl Knorrlander,
Antia Paciotti (Mayor and
his wife), Charles Perrier
and Rosita Arietta (Doctor
and his Wife)

US
Choreographer: Keith Lee
Music: Gustav Mahler (Fifth
Symphony, Adagietto)
Costumes: Marcos Paredes
Premiere: September 26,
1975. Paramount Theater,
Oakland. (A pas de deux
version was first per-
formed: May 6, 1970, Ballet
Theatre Players.)
Cast: Susan Magno, David
McNaughton, Tricia Kaye,
Robert Warner, Laura
Brown, Ron Thiele

LA VALSE
Choreographer: Marc Wilde
Music: Maurice Ravel
Premiere: April 11, 1975. Flint
Center, Cupertino, Calif.
Cast: Tricia Kaye, Ron Thiele,
Carol Rheiner, Robert
Warner, Lynn Pendleton

VINTAGE 70
Choreographer: Jim Piersall
Music: Tape Collage (New
York Rock Ensemble, Step-
penwolf, the Rolling Stones
Costumes: Fran Stephens
Premiere: October 21, 1972.
Oakland Technical High
School Auditorium. (First
performed: 1970.)
Cast: Tricia Kaye, Tom
Crocker, Ron Thiele, Lynne
Laakso, Dianne Brock,
Mindy Berrol, Scott Henry

VISIONS FUGITIVES
Choreographer: Betsy
Erickson
Music: Sergei Prokofiev (Suite
from op. 22, orchestrated
by Rudolf Barshai)
Costumes: Mario Alonzo

Premiere: November 11, 1988.
Paramount Theatre, Oak-
land.
Cast: Abra Rudisill, Joy Gim,
Julie Lowe, Patti Owen,
Susan Taylor, Michael Lowe,
Ron Thiele, Michael Myers,
Mario Alonzo, Jonathan
Brooke

WALK TO PARADISE
GARDEN
Choreographer: Ronn Guidi
Music: Frederick Delius (from
A Village Romeo & Juliet)
Costumes: Virginia Vander-
grift
Premiere: October 15, 1970.
Kaiser Center Auditorium,
Oakland.
Cast: Anita Paciotti, John
Sullivan

WATERWAYS
Choreographer: Betsy
Erickson
Music: Toru Takemitsu
Costumes: Sandra Woodall
Premiere: September 24,
1982. Zellerbach Audito-
rium, Berkeley
Cast: Erin Leedom, Lance
James, Shirlee Reevie, Ron
Thiele, Julie Lowe, Michael
Lowe

WE, THE CLOWN
Choreographer: John McFall
Music: Victor Charles
Costumes: Victoria Gyorfi
Premiere: October 27, 1978.
Paramount Theater, Oak-
land.
Cast: Ron Thiele, Michael
Lowe

XYZ
Choreographer: Michael
Cappara
Music: Sly and the Family
Stone ("Sex Machine")
Premiere: September 23, 1973.
Chabot College Theater,
Hayward, Calif.
Cast: Dianne Brock, Tricia
Kaye, Janet Carole, Michael
Cappara

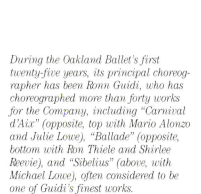

*During the Oakland Ballet's first
twenty-five years, its principal choreographer has been Ronn Guidi, who has
choreographed more than forty works
for the Company, including "Carnival
d'Aix" (opposite, top with Mario Alonzo
and Julie Lowe), "Ballade" (opposite,
bottom with Ron Thiele and Shirlee
Reevie), and "Sibelius" (above, with
Michael Lowe), often considered to be
one of Guidi's finest works.*

The Company's Choreographers: A Directory

COMPILED BY WILLIAM HUCK

The following directory lists those choreographers whose works have been performed by the Oakland Ballet from its 1965 inception through its 1990 spring season. If a particular work was a collaborative choreographic effort, the co-choreographer's name is listed in parentheses.

ARPINO, GERALD
1974 PARTITA FOR FOUR

BALANCHINE, GEORGE
1988 "HAND OF FATE" PAS DE DEUX FROM COTILLON

BEAL, TANDY
1984 . . . THIS HARSH SPECTACLE, THIS INVISIBLE ACTIVITY, THIS SENSE . . .

BLOOD, DAVID
1976 QUIET CITY

BORIS, RUTHANNA
1983 CAKEWALK

BOURKE, WALTER
1975 GRAND TARANTELLA

BURGOON, LARRY
1976 PAS DE TROIS IN A NEO-CLASSIC MODE

BUTLER, JOHN
1985 CARMINA BURANA

CANIPAROLI, VAL
1983 STREET SONGS
1984 TAR MARMALADE
1986 AUBADE

CAPPARA, MICHAEL
1973 XYZ

CARVAJAL, CARLOS
1970 CHIMERA
1977 SHAPES OF EVENING
1983 CRYSTAL SLIPPER
1984 SYNERGIES

CLIFFORD, JOHN
1974 FANTASIES

COMELIN, JEAN PAUL
1981 DAPHNIS AND CHLOE

CONRAD, ARTHUR
1972 DIVERTISSEMENT
1975 A SOLDIER'S TALE (with Ronn Guidi)

DE MILLE, AGNES
1983 INCONSEQUENTIALS
1986 FALL RIVER LEGEND

DELSON, DOLORES
1973 ABRAHAM AND ISAAC

DOLIN, ANTON
1976 PAS DE QUATRE (after Perrot)

ERICKSON, BETSY
1982 WATERWAYS
1983 SONATA
1984 AT A TIME WHEN
1986 SFUMATO
1988 VISIONS FUGITIVES

FEVES, ANGENE
1965 THE PROPOSAL OF PANTALONE

FOKINE, MICHEL
1976 LE SPECTRE DE LA ROSE
1979 SHEHERAZADE
1982 POLOVETSIAN DANCES

FRANKLIN, FREDERIC
1987 GISELLE (after Coralli, Perrot, Petipa)
1988 TRIBUTE

GUIDI, RONN
1965 UIRAPURU
      HANSEL AND GRETEL (with Raoul Pausé)
1966 PETER AND THE WOLF
      TROIS GYMNOPEDIES
      RESPIGHI DANCES
1967 CONCIERTO DE ARANJUEZ
1969 CARMINA BURANA— PAS DE DEUX
1970 CARNIVAL
      FOREST
      HELP, HELP, THE GLOBOLINKS
      LES LESQUERCARDES
      MORNING SONG
      WALK TO PARADISE GARDEN
1971 APOCALYPSE
      REQUIEM
      JOHN FIELD
      QUIET CITY
      SOIREE MUSICALE
      TOUCH
1972 ARMENIAN DANCES
      THE NUTCRACKER
      SEMIRAMIDE
1973 BLUE DANUBE
      CARMINA BURANA
      FRAGMENT
      POLOVETZIAN DANCES
      RAGS
1974 GRAINGER SUITE
1975 JUPITER
      LANDESCAPE
      A SOLDIER'S TALE (with Arthur Conrad)

IRINA NIJINSKA AND FRANK W. D. RIES
IN REHEARSAL OF *LE TRAIN BLEU*,
WITH DANCERS MICHAEL LOWE AND ABRA RUDISILL

THE UNICORN, THE
GORGON, AND THE
MANTICORE
1976 GALLOPS AND KISSES
SEASCAPE
1977 CAMILLE
1978 LES PETITS RIENS
(with Ron Thiele)
SIBELIUS
1980 BALLADE
CARNIVAL D'AIX
EL SALON MEXICO
IN AUTUMN
1981 FANTASIA PARA UN
GENTILHOMBRE
1982 DVORAK DANCES
1985 THE SEASONS,
SELECTIONS (with
Raoul Pausé)
1987 NICHOLAS AND
CONCEPCION,
Excerpts from Act II
1990 PETER AND THE
WOLF

HARMS, RACHAEL
1980 SLOE GIN

JOOSS, KURT
1984 THE GREEN TABLE

KEELER, EMILY
1988 THE AWAKENING

KING, RAYMOND
1972 SILENT SPRING (also
called ENCOUNTER)
HOLBERG SUITE
CONCERTO IN 'D'

KUCH, RICHARD
1982 THE BROOD

LEE, KEITH
1975 TIMES PAST
US

LOPES, DAVID L.
1977 OPUS 29—
IN MEMORIAM

LORING, EUGENE
1976 BILLY THE KID
1977 THE SISTERS
1978 THE TENDER LAND
1980 TIME UNTO TIME

MARCUSS, JUDITH
1974 FUSION

MASSINE, LEONIDE
1978 LA BOUTIQUE
FANTASQUE
1979 SNOW MAIDEN (also
called LE SOLEIL DE
NUIT)

McFALL, JOHN
1978 WE, THE CLOWN
1982 BEETHOVEN QUARTETS
1985 TRIGGER

McNAUGHTON, DAVID
1976 CARMEN SUITE
MANDOLIN DREAMS
1989 GYPSY

MORTIMER, ZELDA
1977 ANOTHER DAY,
ANOTHER DOLLAR

NADEL, IRINE
1976 SANCTUM

NEL, PETER
1976 MOZART FOR EIGHT

NIJINSKA, BRONISLAVA
1981 LES NOCES
1982 LES BICHES
1989 LE TRAIN BLEU

NORTH, ROBERT
1983 DEATH AND THE
MAIDEN

O'DONNELL, MAY
1989 PURSUIT OF
HAPPINESS

PASQUALETTI, JOHN
1974 DUO CONCERTANT
STREETCAR NAMED
DESIRE
1977 DEATH IN VENICE
RESURRECTION
1978 THE RITE OF SPRING

PAUSE, RAOUL
1965 SYLVIA SUITE
HANSEL AND GRETEL
(with Ronn Guidi)
CONCERT WALTZES
(with Marc Wilde)
1985 THE SEASONS,
SELECTIONS (with
Ronn Guidi)

PIERRIER, CHARLES
1973 LOVE IN BATH

PIERSALL, JIM
1972 VINTAGE 70
1973 ROMANIAN DANCES

RUUD, TOMM
1986 BELLA DI NOTTE

SERGEYEV, NICHOLAS
1977 COPPELIA (after Ivanov
and Cecchetti)

SIMMONS, STEPHEN K.
1973 RAYMONDA, CORTEGE
HONGROIS
1974 LE CID
PETRUSHKA

SOKOLOW, ANNA
1980 ROOMS

STEWART, PAUL
1976 RODEO

STREETS, SALLY
1980 PAS DE TROIS
1981 LE SOIR

THIELE, RON
1973 BRANDENBURG
        CONCERTO NO. 2
1974 BRANDENBURG
        CONCERTO NO. 3
        CHACONNE
        THE FOUNTAINS OF
        ROME (with Jack
        Yantis)
1975 CRYSTALS
        RAVEL PIANO
        CONCERTO
1978 LES PETITS RIENS (with
        Ronn Guidi)
1982 AMIS
1983 EPISODES
1987 DIVERSIONS
1989 HOW'D THEY CATCH
        ME?

TUDOR, ANTONY
1988 JARDIN AUX LILAS

WARNER, ROBERT
1976 EL SALON MEXICO

WAY, BRENDA
1987 THIS POINT IN TIME

WEIDMAN, CHARLES
1985 LYNCHTOWN
1986 BRAHMS WALTZES

WILDE, MARC
1965 CONCERT WALTZES
        (with Raoul Pausé)
1966 JAZZIANA
1972 AFTERNOON OF A
        FAUN
1973 CONCERTO GROSSO #1
        IN G
1974 BOLERO
1975 LA VALSE
1978 BRAHMS INTERMEZZI
        THE SIRENS

YANTIS, JACK
1973 PEAR
1974 DENSITY 21
        FOUNTAINS OF ROME
        (with Ron Thiele)
1975 STAR JOURNEY
        TWO OUT OF "FOUR"

Many distinguished choreographers have worked with the Oakland Ballet, including Léonide Massine (opposite, top), Frederic Franklin (opposite, bottom), Tandy Beal (left, top), Kurt Jooss's daughter, Anna Markard (left, bottom), and Eugene Loring, seen here taking a curtain call with the Company.

Photography Credits

The photographs in this publication come from the following collections: the San Francisco Performing Arts Library and Museum (front cover, pages 14, 15, 24, 25 bottom, 27, 32 bottom, 34, 37, 42); the *Oakland Tribune* (pages 10, 18, 20, 25 top); Janice Ross (pages 31, 31 top, 35); Ronn Guidi (page 17); and Ron Thiele (page 38 top). All of the other photographs are from the files of the Oakland Ballet.

Marty Sohl photographed those images on the front inside cover, the back inside cover, and on pages 30, 31 top, 35 top, 36 top, 40, 44 top, 45, 48, 49, 52, 53, 58 bottom, 59, 62, 63 bottom, 66, 67, 69, 70, 73, 74, and 76. Other photographers include William Acheson (pages 8, 38 bottom, 43 top, 68 top); Arne Folkedal (27 top right, 27 bottom right, 37); Harry Wade (43 bottom, 68 bottom), Hazel M. Wintler (10); Regan Jessett (18); Bill Crouch (20 top); John Howell (25 top); Bourret/McAllister (27 left bottom); Herrington-Olson (32 top); Gary Sinick (36 bottom); Ron Thiele (38 top); John Markowski (39, 44 bottom); Lloyd Englert (63 top); and Don Bradburn (73 top). All other photographs are uncredited.

SUSAN TAYLOR IN JOHN McFALL'S *TRIGGER*

Notes

All interviews were conducted by William Huck during the summer of 1990, unless otherwise noted. Tape recordings of many of these interviews are in the collection of the San Francisco Performing Arts Library and Museum.

PRELUDE

[1] Anna Kisselgoff, "Dance: Oakland Ballet in Brooklyn," *The New York Times*, February 13, 1985.

[2] Unsigned news story, *Oakland Tribune*, October 26, 1948. Also Clifford Gessler, "A Stable Turned into Dance Studio," *Oakland Tribune*, August 15, 1948.

[3] Anita Paciotti, interview, July 18, 1990. The physical description of Pausé's studio comes from this interview and Ronn Guidi interviews, June 30 and July 20, 1990. For a contemporary account of Pausé and his work, see *The Trumpeter* 4, no. 4, 7.

[4] The exact date of Pausé's birth is unknown. From the information given in his *Oakland Tribune* obituary on November 19, 1980 (the day following his death), one can conclude that Pausé was born in 1907.

[5] Paciotti, interview, July 18, 1990.

[6] Guidi, interview, June 30, 1990.

[7] Paciotti, interview, July 18, 1990.

[8] "Dancer Will Form Ballet," *Oakland Tribune*, December 2, 1928, says that "Pausé . . . first achieved local notice as a member of The *Tribune* Juveniles some six years ago." This is the closest we have to a substantiation of Pausé's birth date as obtained from his obituary. If Pausé was born in 1907, he would have been a juvenile of fifteen in 1922, just before he returned to Chicago.

[9] For a history of the Pavley-Oukrainsky Ballet, see Ann Barzell, "Chicago's 'Two Russians': Andreas Pavley and Serge Oukrainsky," *Dance Magazine*, June 1979, 63–94.

[10] Guidi, interview, June 30, 1990. See also "Toast for the Twentieth" in Oakland Ballet's 1985 fall program magazine, where Guidi recounts the story in substantially the same words; see also "Local Boy Makes Good," *Glad Rag: News of the Laurel Community* 3, no. 2, October 1979.

[11] Guidi, interview, June 30, 1990.

[12] Theresa Loeb Cone, *Oakland Tribune*, August 6, 1954.

[13] Clifford Gessler, *Oakland Tribune*, April 6, 1957. Whenever Oakland Ballet has provided a brief history of itself in programs, it always dates the formation of the Players Guild in 1954, which is, I believe, the first year Pausé's dancers appeared at the Woodminster Amphitheater, not the year of the founding of the Players Guild. In this 1957 review, Gessler is quite specific in saying that he is reviewing the first performance of a new organization called the Players Guild.

[14] Clifford Gessler, *Oakland Tribune*, April 6, 1957.

[15] A November 25, 1960, program declares this performance the Oakland Civic Ballet's inaugural concert.

[16] Guidi, interview, June 30, 1990.

[17] There is some question about the chronology of Ronn Guidi's choreography in the early sixties. I have used both Guidi's own memory and a repertory list prepared by Betty Lewis in 1979 under Guidi's direction. As an example of the confusion, however, there is an unsent letter signed by Guidi on California Playhouse stationery announcing that the *Harp Concerto* was choreographed especially for a pair of performances Sunday, October 27, and Sunday, November 3, which would place it in 1963. To make matters worse, the *Oakland Tribune* announcement of those two concerts claims that it is *Respighi Dances*, not *Harp Concerto*, that is being premiered. Likewise *Trois Gymnopédies*, which Guidi remembers as first appearing in a studio performance of 1961, is variously dated in those early years as 1961, 1962, 1963, and even 1964.

[18] Guidi, interview, July 6, 1990.

A COMPANY IS FORMED

[1] Besides the Pavley-Oukrainsky company, Pausé's chief work as a dancer was with opera companies, including the Chicago, Manhattan, and Cincinnati. After returning to the Bay Area, Pausé not only formed his own studio and its attendant companies, but he became ballet master of the Pacific Opera Company, the San Francisco Light Opera Association, and the Oakland Light Opera Association.

[2] Theresa Loeb Cone, "Theater to Open Here," *Oakland Tribune*, April 10, 1962.

[3] Brock, interview, July 4, 1990.

[4] Guidi, interview, June 30, 1990. Both Paciotti and Brock confirm Guidi's account. Paciotti, who continued to dance off and on for Pausé, admits to having felt torn between the two diverging organizations, while Brock firmly states that "without Ronn's drive, however, we would probably have just continued to complain and grumble behind the scenes." Paciotti, interview, July 18, 1990; Brock, interview, July 4, 1990.

[5] Articles of Incorporation of the Oakland Ballet Company and Guild. Though these articles were notarized by C. Wadsworth White on September 15, 1965, they were not filed with the State of California until October 28, 1965, partly because the ballet company acted as its own lawyer.

ABRA RUDISILL AND RON THIELE IN ANTONY TUDOR'S JARDIN AUX LILAS

[6] *Dance News*, November 1965.

[7] An example of the unbroken continuity between the Oakland Civic Ballet and the Oakland Ballet is that, until 1985, the Oakland Ballet more frequently dated itself back to 1961, when Ronn Guidi became Pausé's Associate Director of the Oakland Civic Ballet, than to 1965, the actual point of its incorporation.

[8] Ronn Guidi, "A Toast to the Twentieth," twentieth anniversary program magazine, fall 1985.

[9] Paul Hertelendy, "Oakland Ballet Company Seeks New Avenues of Dance," *Oakland Tribune*, October 14, 1965.

[10] Brock, interview, July 4, 1990.

[11] Like so many of Ronn Guidi's ballets, *Hansel and Gretel* has been a constantly evolving creation. At various times the music has included not only Humperdinck, Hérold (orchestrated by Lanchberry), and Grieg, but also Lecocq (*Mam'zell Angot*), Handel (*Love in Bath*, arranged by Beecham), and Glazunov (*Scenes de Ballet* and *The Seasons*), together with unspecified numbers by Donizetti, Telemann, and Rossini-Respighi. Frequently these additions were pas de deux, taken from other ballets, to spice up the cavalcade of dancing that rounds out *Hansel* in true Romantic tradition.

[12] Oakland Ballet press release, dated November 27, 1971, in the files of the San Francisco Performing Arts Library and Museum.

[13] Guidi, interview, July 6, 1990; Brock, interview, July 4, 1990.

[14] Paul Hertelendy, "Ballet Brightens Christmas Season," *Oakland Tribune*, December 21, 1964.

[15] The financial information on Oakland Ballet's first season comes from an accounting page from the Oakland Ballet's MacArthur studio; the performance information comes from a "Fact Sheet, January 1966," found in the same place.

[16] Information concerning Oakland Ballet's earliest activities comes from various papers in the Oakland Ballet Studio. These include a "Statement of Receipts and Expenditures for 1965," an "Information Sheet," dated January 1966, and a Newsletter, vol. 1, no. 1, also dated January 1966. See also "Ballet to Play City Dec. 27," *Fremont News Register*, November 12, 1965.

[17] Paul Hertelendy, "What's in a Name?—It's Still Ballet," *Oakland Tribune*, January 8, 1966.

[18] Guidi, interview, June 30, 1990.

[19] The width of Kaiser stage was itself only twenty-two feet, "a mere grand jété or so wide," as Paul Hertelendy said amusingly in the *Oakland Tribune*, April 4, 1966.

[20] Both the *Oakland Tribune* (February 28, 1968) and the *Neighborhood Journal* (April 3, 1968) carried announcements of the school's opening. These accounts are so similar that they must have come from a now-lost press release from the Company itself. Further information from Guidi interviews.

[21] All of the ballerinas interviewed remarked on Thiele's excellence as a partner, especially the care and facility he had in making their mutual movements polished and graceful.

[22] Information on both Thiele and Lowe comes from personal interviews, as well as Larry Shusan, "The Dance of the Athletes," *Oakland Tribune*, November 28, 1974. For Thiele see also *San Francisco Chronicle*, September 26, 1971, Datebook section, and Pamela Gaye, "Ron Thiele: From Baseball to Ballet," *Dance Magazine*, December 1972, 72–75.

[23] Kaye, interview, July 6, 1990.

[24] Brock, interview, July 4, 1990.

[25] Marilyn Tucker, "A Silly Way to Show Creation," *San Francisco Chronicle*, undated review in the files of the San Francisco Performing Arts Library and Museum.

A HOME THEATER, AN EXPANDED REPERTORY

[1] A variety of newspaper articles document the story of the renovation of the Paramount; these include "What Can Be Done with an Old Movie Palace?", a *San Francisco Chronicle* Sunday *Parade* magazine article, September 9, 1973, and the "Performing Arts have Glittering Eastbay Home," *Oakland Tribune*, September 23, 1979. All the major Bay Area papers carried the Paramount's season announcement, after a press conference on April 16, 1973.

[2] Pamela Gaye's review of Oakland's new production was the highlighted *Nutcracker* review in *Dance Magazine*, February 1974.

[3] "Oakland *Nutcracker* heralds great new interest in ballet," *Montclarion*, December 12, 1973. This article is itself a combination of an article by Oakland Ballet's publicity director for *In Flight* magazine, and an undated press release from the Company.

[4] Guidi, letter to Eleanor Rachel Lyon, undated but from the mid-seventies. See also "Oakland Ballet to Preview First Major East-Bay Nutcracker at City's Annual Christmas Tree Lighting, November 29," undated press release from early November 1973.

[5] For information on the Company's early touring, see Oakland Ballet Guild newsletters from 1973 to 1976. See also an unspecified article, "Alamedan travels near, far as tour director for Oakland Ballet company," in the files of the San Francisco Performing Arts Library and Museum.

[6] This account of Arpino's visit with Guidi is taken from interviews

with Guidi as well as from an article about the company: June Elliot, "Oakland's Ballet Company—Getting Bigger and Better," *Montclarion*, October 16, 1974.

[7] Paul Hertelendy, "Oakland Ballet Produces Rousing *Carmina Burana*," *Oakland Tribune*, May 13, 1973.

[8] Heuwell Tircuit, "Light Diversion from Summer Dance," *San Francisco Chronicle*, August 14, 1978.

[9] Tircuit, *San Francisco Chronicle*, quoted from Oakland Ballet's season brochure.

[10] Stephanie von Buchau, *Pacific Sun*, September 19, 1974, reviewed *Afternoon of a Faun*, calling "Wilde a canny man of the theater. . . . [His] graceful, elegiac choreography and the expertise of the dancers made *Faun* a thoroughly engrossing piece. [Ron] Thiele offered a strong characterization of a half-wild creature stirring with human emotions and executed Wilde's Nijinsky quotes beautifully. Miss Laakso was suitably delicate (even though she has a decisive style and impressive extensions) as the nymph who can't make up her mind."

[11] Whiteside, interview, July 10, 1990.

[12] *The New York Times*, March 18, 1981, and June 3, 1982.

[13] Kaye, interview, July 6, 1990.

[14] Guidi reports that Loring's lasting contribution to him was the older man's firm belief in the narrative art of ballet. At a time when the country was almost completely under the sway of Balanchine's abstract genius, Guidi maintained the viability of dramatic ballet. This characteristic, reinforced by Loring, gave Oakland Ballet a unique and, as it turns out, a prophetic repertory.

[15] Lynn Garafola, *Diaghilev's Ballets Russes* (New York: Oxford University Press, 1989), 336.

[16] Press release, March 25, 1974, in the files of the San Francisco Performing Arts Library and Museum. What pleased the Oakland Ballet most about its new Board of Directors was the Board's diversity of background. "By establishing a community-oriented board, with representatives from varied ethnic backgrounds, age groups and professions," General Manager Ted Lakey announced, "we're hoping to break-down the image of ballet as a white, middle-class art form. We're out to bring dance to all people of the East Bay—encouraging their involvement and participation, as well as support."

[17] Information on the company's size and activities in 1972 comes from the California Arts Council's directory of that year. The 1976 information is most coherently summarized in Oakland Ballet General Manager Stephanie Zimmerman's reports to the Ballet Guild Newsletters. The 1979 information derives from a funding proposal sent out to several perspective sources on December 17, 1979. The growth rate of the budget comes from a report to the Board of Directors by Mark Denton, dated May 26, 1982.

THE NIJINSKA BALLETS AND INTERNATIONAL RECOGNITION

[1] Oakland Ballet's was the first production of *Les Noces* by an American company, but the ballet had been first seen in America in 1936, when it was perceptively reviewed by Edwin Denby, *Dance Writings* (New York: Alfred A. Knopf, 1986), 37–38.

[2] Allan Ulrich, "*Les Noces* triumphs for Oakland Ballet," *San Francisco Examiner*, September 26, 1981.

[3] Walter Terry, "Commentary: The 1982 Spoleto Festival U.S.A.," *Dance Magazine*, August 1982, 78.

[4] Irina Nijinska's characterization of the Oakland company comes from Sean O'Neil, "Bay Area's Best Bets: Oakland Ballet Banks on Adventure," *Lance Magazine*, October 1985, 63.

[5] Thiele, interview, August 14, 1990.

[6] Guidi, interview, July 20, 1990.

[7] Thiele, interview, August 14, 1990.

[8] Tobi Tobias, "Life Studies," *New York Magazine*, March 26, 1990.

[9] Jack Anderson, "With Luck, Revivals Deliver Dividends," *New York Times*, March 25, 1990.

[10] Janice Ross, "Reviews: Oakland Ballet," *Dance Magazine*, February 1990.

[11] *San Francisco Chronicle*, October 25, 1982.

[12] Guidi, interview, July 20, 1990.

[13] Original program, October 26, 1984.

[14] Guidi, interview, July 20, 1990.

[15] Artistic Director/General Manager's Report to the Oakland Ballet's Board of Directors, May 26, 1982.

[16] William Murray, "Remembrance of Things Past," *California Magazine*, September 1983.

[17] Accounting sheet included in "Agenda for the Meeting of the Board of Directors, February 29, 1984."

[18] "Report of the Finance Committee of the Board of Directors, October 21, 1984."

[19] Guidi's characterization of Erin Leedom at fifteen, together with Ruthanna Boris's remark and the final quotation in this paragraph, come from Sean O'Neil, "Oakland's Prima: Erin Leedom,' *Dance Magazine*, October 1985, 66–67.

[20] Paul Parish, "San Francisco Season," *Ballet Review*, Summer 1987, 87–88.

[21] Janice Ross, "Oakland Ballet offers money's worth of premieres," *Oakland Tribune*, October 17, 1983.

[22] Anna Kisselgoff, "Dance: Oakland Ballet in Brooklyn," *The New York Times*, February 13, 1985.

The San Francisco Performing Arts Library and Museum—formerly the Archives for the Performing Arts—is a nonprofit institution dedicated to collecting, preserving, and making available materials on the performing arts. The collection, the largest of its kind on the West Coast, includes both national and international holdings, but focuses principally on the rich heritage of the lively arts in the San Francisco Bay Area—from the rough-and-tumble Gold Rush, through the Great Earthquake, to the current wealth of world-class music, dance, and theater.

Located in the heart of San Francisco's performing arts center, the Performing Arts Library and Museum features more than one million historic programs, photographs, playbills, and press clippings, as well as a core collection of scene and costume designs, fine art, artifacts, videotapes, periodicals, and books, including one of the largest collections of dance materials in the West.

The collection concentrates on those performing arts presented in a live, theatrical venue—music, dance, opera, theater—and documents companies both large and small, art both experimental and mainstream, individual artists as well as major institutions. The multicultural art forms that have long contributed to the diversity of Bay Area culture are also represented in the Library's holdings. The collection is available to the public on a non-circulating basis, for the purposes of research, education, and enjoyment.

The Performing Arts Library and Museum—founded by the late Russell Hartley—is privately funded and depends upon the contributions of its supporters and dues of its members. Membership is open to all. Thanks to its members and supporters, the Library and Museum presents a lively series of publications, exhibitions, and lectures throughout the year.

Through these and other services, the San Francisco Performing Arts Library and Museum hopes to encourage study in all aspects of our performing arts heritage, to foster the exchange of ideas and resources, and, most importantly, to preserve and protect irreplaceable traces of our past as a foundation for future greatness.